How to Be a Great Online Teacher

Kay Johnson Lehmann

ScarecrowEducation
Lanham, Maryland • Toronto • Oxford
2004

Published in the United States of America
by ScarecrowEducation
An imprint of The Rowman & Littlefield Publishing Group, Inc.
4501 Forbes Boulevard, Suite 200, Lanham, Maryland 20706
www.scarecroweducation.com

PO Box 317
Oxford
OX2 9RU, UK

Copyright © 2004 by Kay Johnson Lehmann

All rights reserved. No part of this publication may be reproduced,
stored in a retrieval system, or transmitted in any form or by any
means, electronic, mechanical, photocopying, recording, or otherwise,
without the prior permission of the publisher.

British Library Cataloguing in Publication Information Available

Library of Congress Cataloging-in-Publication Data

Lehmann, Kay Johnson, 1957–
    How to be a great online teacher / Kay Johnson Lehmann.
        p. cm.
    Includes bibliographical references.
    ISBN 1-57886-112-8 (pbk. : alk. paper)
    1. Computer-assisted instruction. 2. Internet in education. 3.
Teachers—Training of. I. Title.
LB1028.5 .L433 2004
378.1'7344678—dc22

                                            2003024415

♾️™ The paper used in this publication meets the minimum requirements of
American National Standard for Information Sciences—Permanence of Paper
for Printed Library Materials, ANSI/NISO Z39.48-1992.
Manufactured in the United States of America.

Contents

Preface

Under the right conditions the correct mix of flour, yeast, sugar, salt, and moisture creates a perfect loaf of bread with a crusty exterior and an interior webbed with tiny holes. When bread rises too fast, large holes develop inside the loaf, sometimes even causing the bread to collapse. The exponential growth of online learning is leaving holes in the bread loaf known as education. Online learning is a relatively new ingredient in this recipe.

Two ingredients are very necessary but are undersupplied in the online educational bakery. The first ingredient is the proper training and support for those who wish to teach successfully online. The second is course design that fully takes advantage of the unique qualities of the online environment. The lack of attention to these ingredients is leaving those gaping holes in the educational bread loaf.

This book deals with the first of those ingredients, the knowledge base and skills to be successful teaching online. The book is designed to supplement and extend training that is already offered by the institution or agency offering the online course.

Rest assured that good teaching is still good teaching whether online or face to face. The qualities that describe good teachers—caring, supportive, structured, and so on—are all especially important in the online world. How that structure, support, and caring are communicated online is the difference.

Acknowledgments

This book would not be possible without those who supported me during my training and subsequent work as an online instructor. In particular, I would like to thank my husband and online teaching colleague, Jim Lehmann, for his unflagging patience, confidence, and support. A big thank you to my wonderful children, Patrick and Megan Bowe, as well as my stepdaughters, Joanna and Sara Lehmann. And a final thank you to my parents, William and Marjorie Johnson. It was only through my family's love and belief in me that I was able to make this leap to the brave new world of online education as well as fulfilling my dream of becoming an author.

I would also like to thank everyone involved in the California State University/Hayward campus master's degree in education/online teaching and learning specialty program, especially Dr. Nan Chico. Additional thanks go to my colleague and dear friend from that master's program Dennis O'Connor, who encouraged me to take the leap out of the K–12 educational environment at the same time he did.

Thank you to Joan Vandervelde for her faith in hiring me to write and teach my first online courses. Joan, I have learned so much from you. A final note of gratitude goes to all my former students and colleagues from the face-to-face educational arena and the online educational realm. Every one of you has helped me to learn and grow as an educator.

1

The Cold, Impersonal Myth

The myth that online learning is cold and impersonal is just that, a myth. Many students, once acclimated to the online environment, find that they participate more, know their colleagues better and discuss the content more deeply than they ever have in a traditional or face-to-face course. One online student and full-time teacher, Angela Gallegos, said, "For this being an online class, you really took the time to get to know us. . . . You are a wonderful teacher who made me feel as though I was in a classroom" (Angela Gallegos, personal communication, August 29, 2003).

Sam Paskey, another classroom teacher/online student, said it this way, "When I was getting my teaching degree I found it very helpful to be able to have class discussions about topics we had to read or watch on video. I am more of a tactile learner and just reading or watching video is not enough for me. I was worried about this type of masters format at first because of not having those personal classroom discussions. I soon found out that the discussion postings we have between each other had the greatest impact on my learning in this course. We have had over 800 postings on twelve topics. I found myself being able to say more things than I could have in a regular classroom setting. I was able to do this because I was able to think my response through before reacting with a response I might not have meant. In a regular classroom you meet for a certain amount of time and I believe we could not have said as much as we did in the online discussions. Overall, I think everyone feels more at ease saying what they truly think in the online format" (Sam Paskey, personal communication, June 18, 2003).

Kevin Click had this to say about these new communication methods used during his first-ever online class, "I have sincerely benefited from the contacts with my fellow classmates. The discussion board activity is new to me, and I find it a very constructive opportunity for idea exchange, sharing of best practices, and conveying classroom anecdotes. I believe that this activity provides a productive medium of exchange not practical or possible in a traditional classroom. Through technology, we have established a learning community with a valuable diversity of background and experience from all regions of the nation. There are many viewpoints to consider with each issue that comes up, and I enjoy the dynamic manner in which we are teaching each other" (Kevin Click, personal communication, June 1, 2003).

Positive, warm, proactive instructor communication is crucial in creating an environment where participants feel valued and safe in developing themselves as online learners. Students have validated this belief many times over. One eager first-time online learner and classroom teacher gushed, "Professor Lehmann, I want to grow up to be just like you! I'm not kidding. I am SO impressed that with all the students you have, you could pull up all that information about me so quickly and respond on such a personal level. Thank you. You are kind and supportive and I appreciate it a great deal especially without face-to-face interaction to ease some of the jitters. I am now looking forward to the rest of the course! Hooray" (Elizabeth Davidge, personal communication, June 26, 2003).

In a letter to the online adjunct faculty of Walden University, Dr. Sheila Bartle, assistant director of the master's in education program, said:

After a year of acting as primary support personnel for the faculty, I'd like to take this opportunity to offer a few personal observations. . . . Distance education certainly offers its challenges, the foremost of which is, of course, the absence of the immediate physical presence of the student to the faculty member and to classmates. Such a lack has profound implications, it seems to me, and I want to applaud you for doing so much to overcome the inadequacies and barriers posed by absence, by the inability to see a face, read its meaning, and respond with all the rich possibilities offered by physical presence . . . you faculty have found ways to convey the power of your commitment to education and your pleasure in their company to these students!

Students applaud your positive and affirming engagement with them . . . and are highly conscious that encouragement is infinitely more effective than negative criticism. You have enabled these adult professionals . . . they thrive on your personal, individualized feedback. (personal communication, September 5, 2003)

According to OnlineLearning.net, a supplier of online courses from the University of San Diego, UCLA, and other institutions, "An online instructor plays a vital role in developing and maintaining an effective online learning environment and must possess a unique set of tools to perform successfully" (OnlineLearning.net, 2003). The OnlineLearning.net site features a self-evaluation quiz to determine "Is Online Teaching For Me?" Check out the quiz at http://www.onlinelearning.net/Instructor-Community/selfevaluation.html.

AUTHOR'S BACKGROUND IN EDUCATION

The comments from former students related earlier in the chapter were gathered in just a one-month time span. Emails and online postings such as this arrive all the time. It is my firm belief that these communiqués do arrive with such regularity because the communication skills vital to my award-winning work as a middle school teacher have been transferred to the online environment. My work in public education, substitute teaching, and then teaching sixth and eighth grade was extremely rewarding. The result was classroom grants, training in technology integration, and ultimately state and national teaching awards. Interestingly, despite the wonderful things coming my way, I found myself living for the summers when I got to teach other teachers.

THE MOVE INTO ONLINE PROFESSIONAL DEVELOPMENT

The realization that my truest educational calling was in teacher professional development led me to the California State University/Hayward online teaching and learning master's degree program. In this online program I studied and was immersed in the world of online learning for eighteen months. When the program was completed I took a leave of absence from teaching middle school and pursued my dream of teaching teachers full time.

It was sheer dumb luck that brought me into contact that first summer of unemployment from public schools with a renowned individual in the field of online learning. My first supervisor in online professional development at the University of Northern Iowa (UNI) was Joan Vandervelde. What an honor it was to have someone of her stature in the field of online learning recognize my abilities as an online instructor before I had even completed my first semester as an instructor at UNI. Joan saw such promise and ability in my work during that first six-week course that she asked me to mentor another new UNI online teacher and course developer before that first course was even complete.

THE NEED FOR THIS BOOK

Since that wonderful beginning at UNI, I have taught for several other institutions. One of the beauties of online teaching is the ability to be flexible and become an adjunct professor for more than one institution. It has been highly instructive in fact to view how several institutions select, train, and evaluate their online instructors. Since instructor communication skills are crucial to the success of a course or program, as stated earlier in the chapter, it would follow that these skills are purposefully taught and instructors supported as they develop these skills.

My research and personal observations have shown that this is rarely the case. Most instructor training programs feature the tools of online learning, not the teaching and communication skills. The developers of these tool-based training programs probably assume, albeit wrongly, that communication and teaching skills can be transferred directly and easily from the face-to-face environment to the online environment. This is not always the case. While there are similarities in teaching within both of these environments there are marked differences as well.

The purpose of this book is to guide and supplement current training programs for online instructors and/or offer a guide for online facilitators to develop and refine these important communication skills on their own.

2

The Development of Online Learning

How did online learning develop and where is it headed? Here is some information that will help build the necessary background to facilitate a discussion about how to appropriately and successfully teach in this new environment. Bear with this bit of history.

DEVELOPMENT OF ONLINE LEARNING FROM DISTANCE EDUCATION: A MICRO–MACRO VIEW

While teaching a face-to-face workshop for teachers one day the question arose, how did I get my start in online teaching and learning? Ah, what a good question! The city in which I live is small, yet is home to three colleges. One is a community college and the other two are private, exclusive (read: expensive) colleges. I needed several courses to complete my Washington state certification as a history/social studies teacher and looked at the possibilities around me. The community college did not offer the necessary upper-level courses. After considering the number of credits needed to complete the certification, I determined it would not be prudent to pay private college prices to take the courses at the other local colleges. My answer turned out to be distance education courses from a variety of universities around the country.

A person in the workshop piped up, "You mean university donations?" My puzzled look was his only answer. He continued, "You know, you sign up for a correspondence course and never complete it, even after asking for an extension. You end up donating the money to the college and never getting the credits you needed."

His glib response highlights the end result for many people. Correspondence courses have had a history of very poor completion rates compared to face-to-face classes. Why is it that so many people never complete correspondence courses? Now the answer is clear to me, but back then it was not.

One course taken to complete my certification was not a traditional correspondence course where one submits assignments by mail and waits for the professor to return them. Instead it was an online course. However, other than reading much of the material online instead of from a packet or textbook and emailing the papers to the instructor instead of mailing them, it was identical to a typical correspondence course offering. There was no interaction with other students in the class, there was little interaction with the professor, the feedback was weak and not generally helpful in fostering my growth as a teacher, and I was on my own to learn the content. Sadly, all of these were characteristics of the correspondence and online courses I took to complete that history/social studies endorsement.

No wonder so many distance education offerings become "university donations." Very little about what we know about true education—the benefits of peer–peer interaction, the importance of timely feedback and assessment by a highly qualified instructor, the opportunity to quickly clarify misunderstood or unclear concepts before building upon those concepts with new material and ideas—virtually none of these were part of the distance education courses of the past.

ONLINE LEARNING NOW

Many, many online courses are now heavily dependent on peer–peer and teacher–student interactions on a regular if not daily basis. This means there are several opportunities to clarify concepts before adding new ideas into the mix. These communication opportunities can include use of an online bulletin board or forum to elicit comments from peers or the instructor and/or emailing or even phoning peers or the instructor directly. A good online course features opportunities to stretch thinking skills and get almost immediate feedback. Course materials can be offered through visual and auditory messages as well as the more traditional text.

ONLINE LEARNING IN THE FUTURE

What does the future hold for online learning? "By all accounts, the 1990s witnessed a revolution in distance education. The growth of the Internet coupled with a growing demand for convenient and flexible access to higher education have brought about the greatest change in education delivery since the first correspondence courses were made available in the early nineteenth century" (American Council on Education, 2000).

According to *Forbes* magazine supplement on e-learning, "E-learning is the fastest-growing and most promising market in the education industry. According to WR Hambrecht & Co., e-learning is poised to explode, and the company anticipates the market to more than double in size each year through 2002" (Hall, 2000).

In 1999 Cisco Systems CEO John Chambers (1999) gave a keynote address that included this oft-quoted statement, "The next big killer application for the Internet is going to be education. Education over the Internet is going to be so big it is going to make e-mail look like a rounding error."

In *Distance Learning: Promises, Problems and Possibilities*, the future possibilities are stated this way, "the need seems to be strong for such programs. According to the American Council on Education, the number of students in distance learning doubled from 1995 to 1998 totaling 1.6 million (Devarics, 2001). Another market forecast says that by the year 2002 there will be 2.2 million students in distance education programs, a full 15 per cent of all U.S. college students (Rochester, et.al., 1999, cited in Dibiase, 2000)" (Valentine, 2002, p. 2).

CORRESPONDENCE COURSES NEVER BECAME UBIQUITOUS—WILL ONLINE LEARNING?

Whether or not these predictions of exponential growth come to pass depends greatly on the type of courses and the quality of instruction offered. There is a reason that the whole world did not replace face-to-face secondary and postsecondary education with correspondence courses. The truth is distance learning has only filled niche markets in the past.

For online learning to become truly mainstream it has to offer the best qualities of face-to-face learning as well as the global focus, convenience, and flexibility that can only happen in the online educational realm. No face-to-face course offers the ability to discuss topics with colleagues in Peoria, Pyongyang, and Prague while dressed in your pajamas without having to pay a babysitter or find parking. All this while being able to work at your best time of day for learning!

The possibilities for online learning are clear. Seeing those possibilities blossom will require more attention to the most crucial aspect of any course, the instruction. A great instructor can make a poor course shine whether it is delivered face to face or online, but a poor instructor can drag down an entire group of learners even if he or she has the best, most enticing materials available. That is not to say that course development and the mechanics underlying the course are not important; they are! However, the linchpin for the success of online education is an understanding, well-trained, highly communicative facilitator who pushes, challenges, praises, and excites a group of learners to their maximum level of achievement.

3

Successful Online Communications

Critics of online learning often state that a lack of human contact is a major drawback of online learning when compared to traditional face-to-face classrooms. To know that these critics are dead wrong, one only has to recall an email that caused the recipient to laugh out loud, or LOL as email users often abbreviate this phenomenon. It is very possible to connect deeply with others whom we have never seen but with whom we share electronic communications. To create these important human connections in the online classroom requires two elements: selection of the proper communication tools for each particular course and good facilitation by the instructor.

COMMUNICATION IS THE DIFFERENCE

Communication is what separates true online learning from web-based tutorials. It is through the use of communication tools that learners are able to connect with other learners and with their facilitator. These tools bring the human, and humane, aspects to the virtual classroom.

The communication tools of online learning will be discussed in this chapter. It is assumed that the reader has some idea about these basic tools so in-depth explanations will not be given. Instead, suggestions for effective uses of these tools will be offered.

TEXT-BASED COMMUNICATION TOOLS

Email

Is there a more ubiquitous form of communication in the twenty-first century? Along with the next tool, threaded discussion forums, email forms the bulk of communication between instructor and student in an online course. Here are some hints for effective use of email to communicate:

1. Check and answer email often; nothing tweaks online students more than to have their emails go unanswered.
2. Create email folders to sort out submitted assignments from messages to be answered. Have a separate folder for each unit; this makes it easy to see if someone has not yet turned in an assignment.
3. Learn to use filters in the email program. One way to do this is to have students put the course number or a symbol, such as an ampersand in the subject line of messages. The filters are then set to sort course email directly into a folder separate from day-to-day email communications from Aunt Martha.
4. Get a separate email account through an Internet service provider (ISP) or a free web-based email account. Use this new account exclusively for online teaching. Web-based email accounts can be checked from anywhere. This is especially handy when the instructor is traveling. However, many web-based accounts have storage limitations. Be aware of the limit. If students are sending big assignments they will have to be downloaded and the emails deleted. Otherwise the remainder of the students will receive a bounce-back or rejection message.

Threaded Discussion Forums

Discussion forums are the most common communication tool in online teaching after email. Threaded discussions are like bulletin boards or the kitchen refrigerator or wherever messages can be left for others. One person leaves a message or asks a question, another person leaves a response to the first message. Here are a few ways to use this tool more effectively:

1. Keeping threads organized is the key to having great discussions. Set up a different thread for each question. Add a new thread if a

new discussion develops and if possible move the responses that pertain to the new idea into the new thread.

2. Always start a course with an introduction thread. Have students answer a specific question as part of their introduction. This makes them more fun to read and peruse. Otherwise they read like name, rank, and serial number. A question to include might be: What is the website you visit the most and why? Or make it a question that helps them begin thinking about the course curriculum.

3. Have a conversational thread where students can share personal thoughts, ideas, and the like. This will help keep the conversations out of the serious discussion threads.

4. The facilitator should not answer every student posting. Let the students discuss with each other. The instructor should interject when:
   a. clarification is needed
   b. the discussion is heading off the subject
   c. the tone is becoming mean-spirited because student opinions are at odds or when a student's posting are being ignored

5. Difficulties like the mean-spiritedness just mentioned should be handled privately. Do this via email or telephone. Be sure to first ask if there is a problem. Many times a mean-spirited response is the result of an unintended slight in the threads. Do not lecture; friendly reminders and suggestions are much better.

6. Try to end every instructor posting with a question. This will help extend the discussion and put the ball back into the students' court where the bulk of the discussion belongs.

Chat

Use of chat is limited in most online courses but it can be a very valuable tool since it offers real-time answers to questions.

1. Only use chat in an online course if a private chat area is available and if the students are bunched geographically, not scattered across many time zones. Privacy is very important. Strangers stumbling into the educational discussion would destroy the give-and-take necessary to have an appropriate discourse. And it is hard for geographically diverse students to participate in a chat; it can be done but it is tricky to set up so that it is convenient for everyone.

2. Have a tightly focused discussion point for the chat session; otherwise it quickly becomes difficult to follow the conversation especially if several people are participating.

3. Consider breaking the class into groups, perhaps geographically for this activity, and use chat for conversations with a small number of people.

4. Remember that one of the advantages of online learning is the anytime learning aspect. Students should not have to reorganize their whole week for one chat session. What seems like a convenient time for the instructor may not be at all convenient for each and every student. Be flexible where possible. Give lots of advance notice so participants can plan around the chat time.

5. Either do not require students to participate in chat sessions or offer alternate assignments for the reasons already stated and because connectivity/computer problems may occur. Some school computers are programmed to prevent the execution of Java script. Most chat session windows are set up using Java script so participants who rely on a school computer for coursework may be unable to access the chat room.

6. One great use of chat is for weekly office hours. Pick a couple of different times each week to be online. Then if students have problems or questions they can meet the instructor in the chat room for assistance.

Instant Messaging

Instant messaging is much like chat in that it is synchronous communication but it is much more private than chat generally because it is most often used one on one.

1. Many of the suggestions for chat apply to instant messaging. This is another great way to hold weekly office hours. Unlike chat the instructor can be using the computer for other tasks during office hours while waiting to see if any students need help. The instant messaging software alerts the user that someone has signed on.

2. Encourage students to use instant messaging to discuss group projects.

3. If a student is having a problem for which a one-on-one discussion may be beneficial, set up an instant messaging session. This is a

great way to work things out and unlike a phone call, there will be a transcript of the discussion when it is completed.

File Transfers

Sending drafts of projects or turning in assignments via file transfers is another form of communication.

1. First of all, encourage students to warn recipients before sending a file via email. Email attachments can carry viruses. Viruses can generate emails from the email address book without the knowledge of the computer's owner. When someone sends a quick "heads up, here comes a file" message then it is very unlikely that the message that follows with the file is a virus-spawned attachment.
2. Make sure that everyone including the instructor is using up-to-date virus protection. Set it to update daily if lots of assignment files are being sent and received.
3. Teach students a naming protocol for assignment files so that the teacher will know at a glance from whom the file came and which assignment it contains. Nothing is worse than opening an assignment file to grade it and not having a clue who sent it. Here is an example of a file naming protocol for a history class assignment involving folk stories. The student's last name comes first, separated by a dot (.) then a short piece of information about the course separated by an underscore (_) and the assignment. Example: Lehmann.Hist101_Folk. By the way, when setting up a file naming protocol do not use slashes (/) in file names. The computer interprets slashes as a pathway to locate files.
4. Encourage students to share drafts of assignments with other members of the class for peer review.
5. If a file is going to be transferred back and forth several times, say as part of a small group project online, have students do a "Save As" and add the date to the name of the file each time they send it. For example, if Maria Cruz is sending Jon Ho a project file it might be named CruzHoProject1.13.02. When Jon sends it back the name will be CruzHoProject1.16.02.

NONTEXT COMMUNICATION TOOLS

Other communication tools that are not text based include audio messages using a microphone and the telephone. Audio messages are not commonly used for a variety of reasons including the size of the files created and instructor unfamiliarity with how to record and attach/send/post audio files. The phone, however, is a communication tool that can be very useful in online education. This is especially true if a difficult situation arises with a student or they are absent from the class for a period of time and not answering instructor emails. A phone call can often clear things up quickly.

Video messages are another possible communication tool if one or more people have a web-cam or other video capabilities. Video messages tend to be very memory-intensive so make sure both parties have the Internet connection speed and computer capabilities to handle video if it is to be a required tool in an online course.

DEFINING THE QUALITIES OF SUCCESSFUL
ONLINE COMMUNICATION TOOLS

Many times online instructors have no choice as to what communication tools will be used for a course. However, there are usually several possible communication tool choices for any particular communication.

How does an instructor know which tool to choose? There are three qualities or characteristics that must be present for a tool to be used successfully in any communication. The tool must be: (1) in the student's possession, (2) reasonably accessible to the student, and (3) operable by the student.

What does this list of characteristics really mean to the teacher? First, if the teacher is in charge of deciding which tools will be used in an online course some judgments have to be made about hardware and software requirements for the course. Those judgments must then be communicated to students before they sign up for the course. For the instructor who has a range of available communication tools, the judgment to be made is which tool will be best to use in that particular situation. If possible, use at least two tools for important messages that need to be communicated to a whole group. For a variety of reasons some students will get the message from one tool, but not the other.

Applying the Characteristics to Email

Applying the list to a simple example, email, may help clarify the characteristics. Virtually every online course states that students taking the course have to have an email account. Here is an analysis of email:

- Possession—Students have to possess an email account to participate in an online course. Those who do not have an email account at all cannot participate. Most people signing up for an online course will have an email account. On the off chance that someone does not have an email account, it is suggested that they be guided to their Internet Service Provider to get an email account or that they sign up for a free web-based email account such as Hotmail, Yahoo Mail, or something similar.
- Accessible—Students have to be able to check their email regularly during an online course. In most courses, near-daily access would be a reasonable request. If a student only has access to an email account via the computer at their mother's house, and they visit mom just once a week, then the tool is not reasonably accessible.
- Operable—Students must know how to receive and send email messages. If they do not know how to run their email program, then it is not operable by the student. Depending on the course, operable may also mean that they can attach documents to an email and that they can download documents sent to them as an email attachment. If attachments are a requirement for a course, this should be stated in the materials list that a student sees before registering for the course.

Applying the Characteristics to Video

Some courses are now requiring that students view online video segments as part of the course materials. Video requires a plug-in, a piece of software that will run the video. Plug-ins can usually be downloaded for free from the Internet if a video program is not already installed on the computer. Video can be very memory-intensive and often requires a minimum connection speed. What does all that mean in plain English? Let's examine it more carefully. Here are the characteristics as applied to video:

- Possession—Streaming video requires that information be downloaded quickly enough that the pieces of information can be reassembled as the video is playing. Otherwise the video will stop and start, like a bad videotape, as the computer waits for more information to come in so it

can play another bit of the video. A student with a slow Internet connection likely will not be able to download the stream fast enough to play the
video continuously. The video will not be in their computer fast enough
to work properly. It cannot then be defined as in their possession.

- Accessible—If the video segment is not streaming, that is, if it is a file
  that will be fully downloaded into the memory of the computer before
  being played, it will take a lot of storage space. Someone whose computer is just about out of space may experience a computer crash trying to download a big file. If the student has a slow Internet connection, the video file may take a long time to download. That is time that
  the Internet connection and possibly the whole computer cannot really be used for anything else. Students who are paying long-distance
  fees or who pay by the minute for their Internet connection will find
  this costly in terms of both time and money. Either way the video is es-
  sentially inaccessible for them.
- Operable—A plug-in is needed to run video. A plug-in is a download-
  able piece of software, generally free, that performs a function. In this
  case it will play the video on the computer screen. If a student is on a
  computer without that plug-in and they cannot or will not download the
  plug-in, the video is not operable by the student.

BEING PROACTIVE

For every tool included in a course these criteria should be considered and a
determination made about whether the tool should be required. Students
should be told up front what tools are needed to successfully complete the
course. For example, if it is decided that streaming video is essential to the
course and will be included, the course description should state the minimum
connection speed that can reasonably handle streaming video and that students will need to possess a video plug-in such as QuickTime or Real Player.

Every hardware/software requirement added to the list limits the potential
market of students. It also increases the number of things to troubleshoot.
Troubleshooting can include both the operation of the tools inside the course
site and students' ability to utilize the tools. The goal of considering these
characteristics is not to eliminate all tools from the course but to proactively
plan for all exigencies before a course begins. Every tool comes with advantages and disadvantages. It is up to the course designer and the instructor to
determine whether the advantages outweigh the disadvantages in each situation. Since communication tools are key to a successful course, examine
them closely using the criteria listed in this chapter.

4

Online Instructor or Facilitator?

Online teacher? Online facilitator? Both terms have been used interchangeably throughout this book. Which is the true role in the online classroom? The answer is both.

Teacher

Just as in the regular classroom much of the important work occurs before class begins. Preparation for the lesson may include setting objectives, gathering materials, and determining the elements of the lesson and how students will be assessed. Even when teaching a course designed by someone else, whether online or face to face, the teacher prepares for the lessons in advance, becoming familiar with the content and determining how student success will be defined.

Much of the preparation work for an online course takes place months in advance. It has been estimated that writing an online course takes 300–600 hours. In addition to the preparation mentioned above, writing an online course includes finding web-based resources, writing lectures or explanations, and designing media to fully utilize the power of online learning. The course design will also define the level of interactivity in the course.

Interactivity plays an important role in an online course. However, the level of interactivity varies from institution to institution and from course to course. In general, a high level of interactivity would include daily interactions from instructor to student and from student to student. The lowest level of interactivity would be a self-paced online course where there is a little, if any, interaction between instructor and students. How much interaction there is in a course defines the facilitator's role.

Facilitator

As stated above the level of interactivity embedded in the course design helps determine the duties of the facilitator. Courses can fall anywhere along the continuum from daily interaction to minimal contact. For the purpose of this book daily or near daily interaction is assumed with the understanding that courses may vary down the interactivity scale from there.

Facilitation is as much art as it is science, just like classroom teaching. In fact, many good classroom teachers will quickly develop into fine on-line instructors. Helping students understand the course materials, drawing out their thinking with carefully constructed questions, and providing support when needed as students work to show competency with the material are all a part of the face-to-face and virtual classroom environments.

The major differences between teaching in the face-to-face classroom and the virtual classroom are how messages are communicated and the need to troubleshoot technical problems. In an online course, the majority of the communication will occur through text. Communication through email, instant messaging, threaded discussion, and chat is written communication. Good technical writing skills are a big plus for the online instructor. However, it is not enough to just be able to guide someone using step-by-step directions. It is also important to connect with students to give the online classroom warmth and a human touch. Adding a touch of humanity and even humor through text is not always easy but it can be done! Some examples will be shared in chapter 5.

Troubleshooting Is Part of the Job

The online facilitator has to be prepared to help troubleshoot technical problems. Often the problem is not the tool, it is the students' unfamiliarity with the tool. In other words, they just do not know how to use it. This unfamiliarity might be anything from not knowing how to attach a document to an email to not knowing how to capture a screen shot to put into an assignment. The instructor needs not only to know how to use all course tools, but also to be adept at describing the procedures to fix the problem. It helps to have several good resources to which students can be directed or that the instructor can utilize to help solve the problem.

Some courses have technical support people to whom both online students and instructors can turn for help. These people can be invaluable. They often have a wealth of information and tips at their disposal. Good technical support takes much of the troubleshooting burden off of the back of the instructor, but even then it is likely that the online teacher will still have to do some troubleshooting. One area that rarely involves troubleshooting skills but instead requires other types of skills are the online discussions.

Benefits of Online Discussions

Online discussions can be the most powerful part of a course. The peer–peer and student–teacher interactions in a discussion forum or chat offer the online learner the ability to learn from the materials and the instructor and also from every single person taking the class. Online discussions have some features that face-to-face discussions cannot match.

The first advantage to online discussions is that the entire discussion is recorded because it is done in writing. Anyone, at any time, can review points made in the discussion by reading back through the discussion forums or the chat archives.

Second, everyone can, and should, participate. Unlike a face-to-face discussion where a few people can dominate the discussion, in the online environment everyone has an equal chance to be heard.

Third, for many people the online environment releases them from inhibitions that keep them from being full participants in face-to-face discussions. Shy people often are emboldened; people with communication difficulties such as speech problems or lack of English-speaking ability can take as much time as necessary to compose their postings. In the online world there are no prejudices based on physical appearance since images are rarely shared and there are usually no face-to-face meetings. In fact, preserving this anonymity may be important to some people, a fact that an online teacher should keep in mind. Any requests to post digital photos of participants should be optional.

GOOD DISCUSSION FACILITATION TECHNIQUES

For most good classroom teachers the following techniques to facilitate a
class discussion may be a review. Running a good discussion online is not
vastly different from running one in the classroom. Still, it is important to
review some basic discussion techniques and then look at how they might
apply in the online environment.

- Ask thought-provoking questions to lead to deeper critical thinking.
- Summarize the discussion to validate the views of people who re-
  sponded so far and encourage others to participate in the discussion.
- Review the points made to encourage additional points or opposing
  viewpoints to be posted.
- Provide group feedback to a small or large group.
- Ensure that no one is being ignored.

What does each of these techniques look like when used online? How
can human connectedness occur in the discussions? The following examples showcase the techniques one by one. Some examples may actually
showcase more than one technique. Look for ways that human connections are made through humor, sensitivity, and warmth.

1. Ask Thought-Provoking Questions to Lead to Deeper Critical
   Thinking

   Instructor posting a response to a group of teachers discussing student records for mobile students:
       "Could student records be put on a 'smart card,' which looks like a
   credit card but holds information? Could they be put in a secure location on the Internet? Could they be transmitted electronically from
   one school to another? I would love to see this group expound on
   these ideas."

2. Summarize the Discussion So Far

   Original instructor posting to the same group of teachers discussing
   student records:
       "Gary, Steve, and Maria noted that getting the records can be
   problematic. Sonya suggested that even if the records with IEP

hadn't arrived yet that the classroom teacher at least be told the nature of the student's special needs. That seems like a very reasonable suggestion! Darlene suggested that students not be allowed to enroll until records are received. What about the rest of you? How could getting student records transferred be improved in your school? Is anyone in a school that has a great method they could share?"

3. Review the Points Made

To many people, summarizing the discussion so far and reviewing the points made may seem to be the same thing. Perhaps. The main difference in the way the author employs them is how and to whom the message is directed. The technique called "summarizing the discussion" validates the people who have participated in the discussion. It is a subtle message to those who have not yet participated in the discussion to get with it and serves as a virtual pat on the back to those who bravely got things going. In this current technique, reviewing the points made so far in the discussion, the topics under discussion are validated and this will hopefully encourage new topics to surface.

Original instructor posting to a discussion that reviews some of the majority points and encourages new points to be made:
"So far several people have mentioned that our students will need these skills when they get to the real world. Others have said that technology improves motivation and interest in the topics. I haven't yet seen this in the thread. One of the best ways to work with a negative person is to invite them into the classroom to see students using computers to work on reading, writing, math, and more. If technology is truly integrated, then it is just one of many tools being used in the classroom. Has anyone tried a direct invitation? What were the results? Would this work with teachers who are computer-phobic? Are there some other ideas to share that haven't yet surfaced besides my suggestion of a direct invitation?"

4. Provide Group Feedback

Sometimes it is important to respond to the entire learning community in mass, rather than as individuals. What follows is an example of providing group feedback.

Instructor response posting to a small group learning a new teaching technique:

"I am so impressed with this whole group, your enthusiasm, ideas, and willingness to try new things. Speaking of trying new things. . . . In Lesson 2 we will be using a technique called Think-Pair-Share."

5. Ensure That Everyone Is Involved

Watch the threads to make sure that every person has had a response to their original posting. It can be hurtful to post a message and have no one respond to it. The instructor should respond to any original postings that have gone unnoticed for more than two days. Another method of making sure students are not ignored by their peers is to direct students to a posting that has gone unnoticed or which has not yet been fleshed out through discussion.

Original instructor posting that directs others to fellow students who are inadvertently being ignored or whose points need to be fleshed out:

"Cleo and Gary have both said they don't have an ESL population or ESL resource people. What advice could those of you who do work with ESL students give them that they can file away for that inevitable day when an ESL student does arrive in their schools?"

WORKING STYLES

In actuality it matters not what tools are used but how those tools are used. In the next chapter some specific suggestions about personalizing and humanizing communications will be shared. That chapter includes some different communication scenarios and some possible responses to each scenario. Before getting to those more specific strategies an overall look at the possible working styles of online instructors is in order.

Most teachers create a personable atmosphere in their face-to-face classrooms that invites the kind of discourse necessary for true learning. The online instructor needs to humanize the online classroom just as he or she would in the face-to-face classroom. The methods used and the depths to which each method is used depend on the type of online class and the level of facilitation to be offered. Potential online instructors might be asking, "What types of online classes are there?" An overview of the types of online classes is called for here.

TYPES OF ONLINE COURSES

Online courses cannot be pigeon-holed into neat categories. Some categories can be used to help define the types of courses offered online. Course types vary in:

1. level of expected facilitation
2. level of peer-peer interactions
3. expected outcomes
4. start–end and assignment due dates
5. involvement of the sponsoring entity or institution.

Table 4.1 describes five possible models. These are generalized to some degree and a particular course may have features of more than one model.

EMPLOYER EXPECTATIONS

The online instructor has to balance several factors. Two of them are common to any type of instruction and no additional explanation will be offered. These are the type of learners to whom the course will be taught, including their level of sophistication and technical knowledge, and personal teaching style. The third factor is somewhat different in the online environment, this is the expectations of the employer or entity offering the course. In an online course the instructor may never meet face to face with the employer.

Special attention has to be given to learning the expectations of the employer if a face-to-face meeting does not occur. These expectations are often clarified during required online instructor training. Even experienced online instructors are often subjected to these required training sessions when employed by a new institution. This can be irritating to veteran online teachers but it does offer a chance to learn the expectations of the new employer. Some things an online instructor new to an organization should ascertain appear on page 28.

Table 4.1. Types of Online Courses

Course Type	Description	Instructor Interaction Level	Peer–Peer Interaction Level	Expected Outcomes	Start–End Dates	Institution or Entity Involvement
Online Tutorial	Instructive webpages that allow a completely self-paced and self-operated journey through the material. Assessment may be built into the tutorial.	No instructor interaction. There may be a Help or Support button but these are generally for technical difficulties, not questions about the course materials.	No peer–peer interactions	Student learns the skill or content knowledge on his or her own. Mastery is dependent on the student's success interacting with the course materials.	Usually completely self-paced. The student can choose when to start, how long to spend on any section and whether or not to complete the course.	Sponsoring agency or individual provides the information as a service to journey customers or to gain traffic to their site. There is usually no charge, no oversight, and no credit/certification granted.
Self-Paced Course	Course through which a student can progress at his or her own choosing. Assessment may be built in or there may be instructor assessment of student work.	Some instructor interaction with the learner may occur particularly at checkpoints and at the end of the course. Some self-paced courses have automated assessment and	Usually there are no peer–peer interactions. It is possible that learners in the course may interact through a bulletin board. Since students are very likely studying different	Student learns the skill or content knowledge on his or her own or with minimal assistance from an instructor. Mastery is determined by checkpoint assignments or	Same as the online tutorial unless the student has to wait for an instructor to assess assignments before proceeding.	Sponsoring agency or individual may provide the information as a service to customers or to gain traffic to their site. In many cases there is a charge, and

		no instructor–student interactions occur.	topics at any one time it is unlikely that substantive discussion of the course topics will take place.	assessments.		credit/certification could be granted.
Asynchronous Cohort Course	Course with fixed start and end dates so that a group of students can go through the course as a cohort group. Assessment may be built in but there may also be instructor or peer–peer assessments of student work. Discussions and other interactions are generally asynchronous so that within parameters the learner completes the work on his or her own time schedule.	Instructor–learner interactions are substantial in this model and may begin with an introduction or orientation to the course site or the course expectations. The instructor usually responds to public and private communications from the learner and assesses work submitted for the course.	The cohort model is designed for peer–peer interaction and support. Requiring all learners to begin each learning module on the same day helps to assure that work and discussions are focused on the content. Learners may interact in real-time synchronously but most interactions will be asynchronous.	Student learns the skill and content through interaction with the course materials and through interactions with peers and the instructor. Peer interactions can add new perspectives or push learners to higher levels of thinking as well as introduce them to additional resources.	The entire cohort group begins on the same day and proceeds through the course modules at about the same pace. The time of day or day of the week in which work is completed is still completely left up to each individual learner but assignments generally have fixed due dates and there is a specific course ending date.	This is very likely a moneymaking endeavor for the sponsoring agency or institution. Credit/certification will generally be granted to all learners who complete the course.

continued

Table 4.1. Types of Online Courses (continued)

Course Type	Description	Instructor Interaction Level	Peer–Peer Interaction Level	Expected Outcomes	Start–End Dates	Institution or Entity Involvement
Synchronous Cohort Course	Course with fixed start and end dates so that a group of students can go through as instructor-led cohort group. Assessment may be built in but there may also be instructor or peer–peer assessments of student work. Some or all discussions and other interactions are synchronous, meaning all learners must be present at a certain time to participate through chat, conference call, video conferencing, or	Same as Asynchronous Cohort Course with the addition of synchronous discussions.	Same as Asynchronous Cohort Course with the addition of peer–peer synchronous interactions.	Same as Asynchronous Cohort Course.	The entire cohort group begins on the same day and proceeds through the course modules at the same pace. This may include assignments that are to be submitted synchronously.	Same as Asynchronous Cohort Course.

instant
messaging.

Hybrid Course	Course with online and face-to-face components. Learners are expected to participate in both the online portions of the course and attend the face-to-face meetings. This model is becoming increasingly common for K–12 online education. This model could have attributes of any of the first three types of online courses, including the use of online tutorials.	Instructor–learner interactions are substantial. They include face-to-face meetings as well as online communications. Instructor assessment of work is the norm.	This characteristic varies depending on the type of online attributes chosen for the course. If the course is designed as an online tutorial with face-to-face meetings with an instructor there may be little or no peer interactions. The level of peer interactions increases if peers are expected to attend the face-to-face components at the same time and increases further if there are online discussion tools used between the face-to-face meetings.	Student learns the skills and content knowledge through his or her own work as well as interactions with an instructor and possibly with a peer group. If peers are involved the outcomes can include characteristics similar to Asynchronous/Synchronous Cohort Courses.	This attribute can vary greatly. In some places this mixed model is used to replace traditional instruction or provide remediation. It may be arranged completely at the convenience of the instructor or may have fixed start and end dates and assignment due dates. Generally if there is a cohort group taking a hybrid class there are fixed start–end dates.	This may be a moneymaking endeavor for the sponsoring agency or institution. It also may be remediation so that credit for failed classes can be granted or the course may be offered to provide specific training for employment. Whether or not credit/certification will be offered depends completely on the reason the hybrid course is being offered and the type of agency involved.

- What are the expectations for frequency of communications with students in the discussion forums and via email?
- What type of feedback is the instructor expected to provide on assignments?
- What are the grading procedures for the institution or entity, including where are grades to be posted for student viewing and how are final grades to be submitted?
- Who is the point of contact if technical questions arise?
- Who is the point of contact about content or pedagogical matters?
- Can course materials or assignments be adapted by the instructor?
- What are the institution's policies for academic integrity, withdrawals, or assigning an incomplete grade?
- What is the anticipated time commitment?
- Last but definitely not least, what are the typical class sizes and what is the pay structure? Is the pay structure tied to course size? How does the instructor arrange to get paid for his or her work when the course ends?

TIME COMMITMENT

Time commitment is mentioned as a significant element. It is important to understand that the time commitment is dependent on many factors. The first of these is the familiarity of the instructor with the course materials. The first time through a course everything always takes longer than in subsequent sessions of the same course. Another factor is the speed at which the instructor reads. Seriously! The majority of information in an online course is text-based. The faster the instructor can read, the more efficiently the work can be completed. The same goes for typing speed. Unless the facilitator is using a voice-activated system for word-processing such as Dragon Naturally Speaking, the ability to type quickly speeds up the rate at which work can be accomplished.

Type of Course

The time commitment is also dependent on the type of course being taught. As seen in table 4.1, the level of instructor interaction with the learner depends on the type of course. And within those models there is still considerable leeway. For example, a course that is part of a degree program may have multiple papers that are to be graded during a term while an isolated professional development course will generally have fewer items to grade. And these items may be projects that can be less time-consuming to grade. The time saved during grading of the projects may be overshadowed by the time spent downloading them depending on the type of project being evaluated.

Assessment

Assessment of projects, papers, and student participation will be markedly easier if rubrics are used as part of the scoring process. More information about rubrics, grading, and assessment in general will be covered in chapter 9. Also, the time commitment can be reduced through increased efficiency. Tips to help online instructors become more efficient and organized will be shared in the next chapter.

Full or Part Time

One final factor that relates to time commitment is whether online teaching is full-time work or if it is part-time employment sandwiched into an already busy life. Online teaching can be a terrific part-time job. The work can be done at any time of the day or night and at any location that has an Internet-capable computer. And, while time of day does not matter, it does matter that a little time be set aside every day during a course to answer questions from students or to respond to postings and assignments. The obligation to be available on a regular basis will be discussed in more detail at the end of the next chapter. Complimentary students often mention instructor availability as one of the characteristics of a good online facilitator.

CHARACTERISTICS OF GOOD ONLINE INSTRUCTORS

Self-Motivated

Good online instructors are self-motivated. There is no need for an alarm clock if online instruction is a full-time job because the instructor can choose when to complete his or her work. Some people work well when determining their own deadlines and pace. Others need the pressure of coworkers and bosses to keep them going. For most online instructors there are very few, if any, coworkers and the boss may be a world away. Therefore it is very important to be self-motivated when working in the online realm.

Human Interaction

Occasionally the author is asked, "How can you work in so much isolation? Don't you go crazy without some kind of human interaction?" The truth is that some people work more productively in a quiet environment. Those people make very good online instructors. And while sanity may still be in question, there is plenty of human interaction throughout the day. Emails, discussion postings, and phone calls are all person–person interactions even when they occur asynchronously. The most important aspect of any human contact is the level of communication. With the right skills the communication level can be quite high using text-based asynchronous tools. Chapter 5 will discuss how to create empathetic, humane, personalized interactions with students in the online classroom.

5

Specific Techniques for Positive Online Interactions

PEOPLE

People take online classes. That may seem like it is too elementary or too basic a statement to make but many students in online courses feel they are treated like numbers, or worse, nonentities. Establishing warm, human connections is a key to retaining students in classes, getting repeat business, and generating positive word of mouth from current students to future students. The skills to develop those human connections are not often taught to online instructors and may not come naturally to those more familiar with face-to-face teaching. A major reason for this book is to help online instructors improve their communication skills.

THIS IS A BUSINESS

The fact is that online courses are a business for most institutions. This is especially true for those organizations that hire instructors. While most instructors in online courses do not worry about retaining students, generating positive word of mouth, or other facets of marketing, they should. Stable, growing programs provide consistent employment and opportunities for pay raises. The alternative is inconsistent employment or pay cuts when programs are fading.

FEELING GOOD

Consistent, well-paid employment is important, yet in all honesty most instructors enjoy having happy customers/students. The majority of instructors will be more motivated by the good feelings that come from positive interactions with their students than the idea of stable employment.

How might those good feelings be communicated? Students who feel positively toward an instructor will often state their pleasure directly to the instructor. People rarely relate their displeasure to an online teacher unless they are really ticked off or a great deal of trust has been established. Satisfied online students will recommend the teacher's classes to other potential students. They will discuss with colleagues in the class their good experiences in private student–student communications. The flipside of this is a private airing of ill will, something the author has nicknamed "the underground rumble." This is when negative student–student communications occur behind the instructor's virtual back. The rumble will be discussed in more detail later in this chapter. Following the advice in this book, hopefully you will be able to develop the deep level of trust necessary for honest communications with online students who will then express directly their occasional frustration.

DIFFERENCES BETWEEN TEXT-BASED COMMUNICATIONS AND FACE-TO-FACE COMMUNICATIONS

So where to begin with developing good communication techniques and patterns? First of all, it is important to recognize how text-based communications differ from face-to-face communications. The majority of communications in online courses are text-based: email, discussion forums, chat, instant messaging, and comments on assignments are all text-based communications. It is possible to include audio or video communications in an online course but these are still rarely used in online courses. Audio/video does allow the learner to hear the inflections and tone of voice; video even includes facial expressions and body language. Compared to audio/video or face-to-face communications, text-based messages seem cold and harsh, leading to the myth about online courses as impersonal. Without some effort, and a few tricks on the part of the message sender, messages can often seem more like a slap in the face to the recipient than a soft caress.

Let's look at text-based communication from another angle. Every reader of this book can remember a book or article that caused him or her to laugh out loud, or one that created a lump in his or her throat. In fact, one of the first communicative acronyms created by early email users was LOL, which stands for laughing out loud. Therefore it is obvious that not all text-based communications feel harsh or lack emotion. It is important to create messages that caress, tickle, or draw a tear from recipients in an online course to reinsert the human connectedness that may otherwise be missing.

HUMOR

One of the first things that most online instructors-in-training are told is, "Humor doesn't work. Don't even try to be humorous in your communications." At least this was the advice given in several training sessions in which I took part. That advice was difficult to reconcile with my personality and the observation that emails from family and friends often required a reply of LOL! Humor does work. It must be handled with care, but it can and does work.

It Has to Be Natural

Those people who do not naturally use humor in daily verbal communications should not attempt it in written communications. Humor cannot be forced. It needs to be a part of the message author's natural personality in order to have it work well in text. A fine online instructor, Walter McKenzie, introduced one method of inserting naturally humorous messages to the author. Walter used tag lines after his signature when posting to the discussion board. Here is an example modeled after Walter's method:

I can't find the email address of the ESL expert that I wanted to try to put you in touch with, darn it! I wish I could have found that old email. Signed, Kay *who is covered in virtual dust from rummaging around in old email folders*

Poke Fun at Yourself

The second piece of advice is that the instructor should poke fun at himself or herself. It would be highly unusual for someone to be offended by a message in which the author was the buffoon. Here is an example of an email message meant to be humorous but still get a point across to the class where the author pokes fun at herself:

Good gravy, did you see the spelling and grammar errors in my last email? Yikes! I know that I should compose in Word, use spell check then copy/paste it into the courseware email system. I must need more coffee this morning! Oyyy!!!

No Sarcasm

While humor can work in text-based communications, sarcastic humor does not. Never try to use sarcasm as humor in written messages. Sarcasm relies heavily on voice inflection to indicate the message is supposed to be taken differently than it appears. Many individuals, including second-language learners, have difficulty with sarcasm even when it is spoken. Here are some examples of attempted sarcasm. Note the way smiley faces, or emoticons, are utilized to indicate the messages are meant to be humorous.

Instructor response: Whichever project you choose, please make sure you LOOK at the rubric for the project in the Assignments/Week 3 information. What I have seen happen in the past is that people use a project they previously created or they have a great time making something new but don't compare it to the rubric and end up with a very low score. Strange as this may sound, I use the rubrics when grading the projects. Isn't that crazy?! ;-)

Instructor response as part of an email directing a student to a folder in a course site: There are tech plan links in the Week 5/External Links folder called, this is going to sound crazy, Technology Plans ;-)

Just think, you only have 2 discussions and 1 real paper left to write for 6661 . . . plus the website, plus the revised concept map. . . . OK, well, we are almost there. The end is in sight! Or is that site? Get it, website. . . . Yeah, I know that was a bad one. ;-)

Peer–Peer Communications

Advice about the use of humor in written communications applies not only to the instructor but also to the students in their peer–peer communications. It will be important for the instructor to offer guidance. How and when to provide that guidance is the question!

If the advice about how to appropriately use humor in course communications is given too early, it may hinder students in developing a friendly rapport. They may be so cautious that their communications become stilted. My advice is to provide guidance about humor in communications if a peer–peer posting or email message looks like it could be misconstrued or if a particular student is developing a pattern that has not yet, but may, prove troublesome.

In the first case, where a message looks like it may be hurtful, private emails to both students should be sent. This lets the message author hear the instructor's thinking about his or her message without losing face in front of the group. It also reassures the recipient that the instructor is looking out for everyone. Many times the victim of the hurtful message will later relate that this reassurance from the instructor at that point kept him or her interested in participating in the class. It doesn't take much negativity in an online course before some people will drop the course entirely. At the same time the private messages are sent, a very carefully worded all-class note should be sent. If this is not done an underground rumble may begin to occur. Here is an example that could have started an underground rumble. The responses sent to the individuals and the group have been included here:

Message from student named Jo, to another student named Jim:
"Boy, I can tell you're from the country Jim! I can see the dust on your cowboy boots from here! That would never work here in the city. You should come visit the big city sometime and see what we see! Then you'd think differently. Signed, Jo"

Teacher response to Jo:
"Differences in viewpoints are very welcome in our discussions; in fact, they strengthen the discussion and take it to higher levels. When issuing a different opinion, make sure that you don't appear to be attacking or making fun of the person with the other viewpoint. It is very easy to have a message be misunderstood in this text-only environment and what might be humorous in a fact-to-face conversation can be viewed as highly offensive in this setting. You'll want to make sure that Jim understood the true intent of your message and that he wasn't offended by it."

Teacher response to Jim:
"Hi Jim, I just wanted to make sure that you weren't offended by the comments that were made in the forum today. I think that Jo is a josh-around kind of guy and I am sure that was the intent of his message. I can understand, though, if you were offended or upset by them. I have communicated to him

that he needs to be more careful about the way messages are worded. Please let me know if you have any concerns because of Jo's message."

Teacher response to the whole class:

"Differences of opinion in our forum can be very healthy to developing a good discussion. It helps us to see other perspectives and to evaluate our own beliefs. Please make sure that it is always clear that you are disagreeing with an opinion, not with the person himself or herself. And please be sure to craft your messages carefully to avoid offending anyone. Humor in a text-based environment can be a tricky thing. Use emoticons such as smiley faces or other ways of showing that something is meant to be funny. Let's continue to have great, wide-open discussions and keep the focus on the issues, not on the people. OK?!"

The Underground Rumble

What is the underground rumble that has been referred to several times in this chapter? This phenomenon occurs when students in a class start communicating privately via email, phone, or in person to gripe or grumble about the course or the instructor. Said another way, the students talk behind the instructor's back. The rumble can be quite damaging to the class morale, but the instructor is often very much unaware that this flurry of communications is occurring. As the online teacher, the best thing to do is prevent the rumble from ever starting by encouraging students to communicate openly whenever there is a question or problem. It is when students are intimidated about asking questions, or questions go unanswered, that the rumble generally begins. And since the rumble communications are done in private it is unlikely that an instructor will find out about the underground rumble unless a student contacts the instructor directly to pass along his or her concerns.

ULTRAPOSITIVE IS BETTER THAN HUMOR

What works even better than humor? Being positive! It is important, very, very important, to maintain a positive tone and outlook in all instructor communications. Most of my online courses involve technology integration into the classroom. Occasionally someone in my class is not terribly proficient with technology and begins to wish the instructor was looking over their shoulder instead of reading their emails and they want to give up and quit. An experienced classroom teacher, but a technology novice, who lived halfway around the globe was one person for whom this technique worked well. The author showered her with glowingly positive emails such as this one:

Instructor response: "Wow! This is great! I know you said it's only partially completed, but look at how much you accomplished on your own before you had to ask for help! I am so impressed with your progress!"

This student one day replied with a message to the effect that she knew exactly what the instructor was doing with all the positive talk. She could see that the messages were designed to build up her self-confidence in her own abilities and, even though she knew exactly what was occurring, she said, "It's working."

So even an experienced classroom teacher who had used positive reinforcement many times in her own classroom saw through the semitransparent positive messages in my communications and still fell prey to this tactic. Like she said, it works! Here are some additional example messages with very positive tones:

Instructor sends out announcements identifying the members of small groups for cooperative work.

Via email, one student asks: "How did you decide on these groups?" That was the entire message along with the student's signature.

Instructor response:

> Good question! I must have forgotten to put that in the message in which I introduced the groups.
>
> I used the survey that everyone filled out before the class began to try to get an idea of tech skill levels. Then I tried to put people together by the grade or subject they teach. . . .
>
> I hope this helps out! I work really hard to balance things but at the suggestion of previous groups I do it earlier in the class so I have less personalized knowledge of each individual and their working style.
>
> If there is a problem I would like to know about it. I have been known to do some rearranging but I hesitate to do it until the groups give working together a try. It is a rare occurrence that I move someone out of or into a group but I have done it.
>
> Thanks for asking a great question!

TIME TO ANSWER

Except in a rare instance when using chat/instant messaging, the online teacher has time to respond to student communications. The student generally has no idea when their message was read. The online facilitator can use this time advantageously. This is especially true if a comment has struck a nerve. Unlike a face-to-face comment that has to be dealt with on the spot, online communications give the advantage of time to craft the response. This thinking period before responding should not be excessive but an overnight delay may give an appropriate amount of time to take a deep breath, write, rewrite, then send a response that will not be regretted or misunderstood. Here is an example of a difficult to answer communication that required some thinking time:

Sent via email to the instructor from a student confessing his difficulties with writing. His original spellings have been left intact:

"I read your comments about my writing and I agree. I must contests to you that I have a profound disability when it comes to writing. You see, I'm a hillbilly from Kentucky! Also I have been teaching children that spell was "wuz." God help us all. Talk to you later."

Instructor response:

"Well then there is a lot of room for improvement isn't there? How exciting for both of us! We will just work together to see how far we can get before the course ends. OK?!"

Once in a while a message arrives that is not irritating. Instead it is just difficult to answer in a positive way. Here is an example of a message that had the author wondering how to answer it in a positive, yet truthful, way:

Instructor email to a student who has posted an assignment before the week even begins and for which the instructor has just posted some additional requirements:

"I saw this morning when downloading files that you had already completed the paper for next week. Wow! You are really on top of things. I must apologize to you because I may be causing you some additional work. Just what you needed, right?! I just now posted the APA formatting requirements for next week. I try to do this before the previous week ends, just in case anyone is trying to get a jumpstart on the next week like you did. I failed to get that done before the week began.

You should look over the APA formatting posting I made in the Q & A forum and double-check that your paper meets those requirements. I apologize. I know how busy teachers are and how badly we all sometimes need to get a jump on things."

TAKE RESPONSIBILITY FOR EVERYTHING

Along with always being positive, there is a related tactic that should be employed. Take responsibility for everything. To the point of being smarmy! Seriously! Take responsibility and be positive. This advice was shared with a new online teacher as part of the mentoring process. It was obvious from her original reply that she was not sure this was the right way to go. Before the first week of her course was over though, she employed the "Take responsibility, stay positive" approach. She emailed quickly after receiving the student's reply to her "I take responsibility" message. "It works! It really works!" she said.

Ultimately, the instructor is responsible for everything about the course. Students do not want to hear excuses; they want someone to take responsibility. Even more so than in a face-to-face course, students hold the online teacher responsible for every part of a course: the course materials, all the links, assignment choices, and the like. Perhaps this is so because the only real point of contact most students have in an online course is the instructor. While clearly the instructor is not responsible for everything, buck-passing is not the way to go. Here are some examples of taking responsibility even when the instructor knows this is not really his or her weight to shoulder:

Comment about the author from a student who just completed a course making a comparison to other online instructors she had experienced:

> This class would never have been so successful without your stewardship. Only names, no faces (except for Dutch the cat) and with very brief biographies, you were able to bring us all together to form a very cohesive group, not an easy task. You brought humor, gave direction, and kept us grounded as we methodically tackled each assignment. You never hesitated to give assistance with personal or technical difficulties. My experience in the past with online courses was "you were on your own," "don't bother me," "no replies." This course restored my faith in online courses.

Comment from a former student who is now in another instructor's class: "We still miss you very much! In a pique of frustration, I am writing you to complain that I still have eight outstanding grades for which I am waiting (from her current instructor). We miss your consistency and your regular feedback."

SHEEPISH STUDENTS ARE QUICKLY WON OVER

My experience over and over again has been that when the instructor takes responsibility for something that is really the student's fault it will be appreciated. Often students will sheepishly admit afterward that whatever occurred was in reality their own fault. Generally, that sheepish student will be so grateful at not having an accusatory finger pointed at them that he or she becomes a model student from there on out, if not an out-and-out cheerleader.

ANSWERING STUDENT COMMUNICATIONS

It should be noted overtly that this chapter is written with the expectation that student communication will be promptly answered. This is not a universally held expectation as evidenced by this comment from an online student:

Comment about another instructor sent via email: "I took an online class. It did not require all that this class does; we simply wrote responses to questions and sent them as an attachment. I had numerous questions for clarification because the syllabus was poorly organized. I emailed him 5–6 times. The class assignments were due each week. Without clarification some of my assignments were graded low. He never did email. I had to call him on the phone."

WOULD THE FACE-TO-FACE INSTRUCTOR IGNORE A STUDENT'S QUESTIONS?

Let's look at this from another angle. The teacher in a face-to-face classroom knows when a student has a question. This might be indicated by the student raising his or her hand, hanging back at the end of class, or visiting the teacher in his or her office during office hours. One way or another, the student gets a chance to ask a question and he or she has a reasonable expectation that there will be an answer from the instructor who is right there in front of him or her. The answer might be "I don't know," but if the teacher fails to answer the question and the student is totally ignored by the teacher, the student will be insulted and hurt by this patently rude behavior.

It is hard to picture an instructor in the face-to-face scenario completely ignoring the student, isn't it? We all know it would be incredibly rude not to answer the question or to state, "No questions will be taken." Yet many online students report that this is a common occurrence in some online courses:

Email from a former student: "Kay, I don't know if anyone from the group has already emailed you, but some of us are pretty upset. We have not heard one word about the papers submitted so far and it is the beginning of Week Three. No feedback on the writing. Is this normal? Signed, Upset and Confused"

Response from the instructor: "Hmmm, is it normal? I don't think so. Is it ideal? Definitely not. But have I heard similar things from previous students? Yes, I am afraid that I have. I hope that you have done your best to contact the faculty member and ask for feedback . . ."

Return response from Upset and Confused: "Kay, thank you for the 'prompt' and honest reply. I haven't emailed and asked for a response from him; I was feeling timid and figured I would hear something. I will try that and let you know how it goes."

Students as our customers, as people, deserve to have their questions answered, and answered in a reasonable amount of time. This is a major responsibility of teachers. Perhaps it is because my background is in K–12 education but it is hard to imagine ignoring a student's questions or refusing to take questions in the first place. Parents would have been knocking on the principal's door if such rude behavior happened in my middle school, and rightly so!

ANSWERING QUESTIONS WHILE ON THE ROAD

The author's personal standard for answering email is that every query is answered within twenty-four hours. Sometimes the answer is, "I will have to get back to you on that." That response at least informs the student that their email has arrived and been read. Once in a while there are periods of inaccessibility when traveling. Students are told this in advance and encouraged to contact one another for help until the instructor is back online. In the author's opinion it is not conscionable to be out of contact for longer than at most a few days during a course. Even while traveling, there are public libraries and cyber cafes where email can be answered. Those of us who have made online teaching our full-time job often have invested in a laptop computer for access to courses and email while traveling. If students are expected to be responsible for responding to discussions and completing assignments while traveling, then the author believes that we as professional educators must hold ourselves to that same standard.

6

Tips to Increase Efficiency

During student teaching in a regular K–12 classroom most preservice teachers find that it takes them hours to accomplish what their master teacher gets done in minutes. This is because the student teacher lacks two things: practical experience and the specialized knowledge of the job. In any endeavor, things tend to go smoother and quicker with some practice or experience. In addition, some of the workload will be lessened when the student teacher picks up the little tips and tricks that allow the master teacher to be more efficient. These are the tricks of the trade, as they could be called, or the specialized knowledge, as they are referred to here.

The same could be said about learning to be an online teacher. At first the facilitator is inexperienced and slow. Some things just require practice. There is no substitute for these experiences and they certainly cannot be put into a book. However, the specialized knowledge, the tricks of the trade, which improve instructor efficiency, can be put in a book.

This chapter features some ways that this author has been able to successfully teach multiple classes and still take the time to make those all-important human connections discussed in the last chapter. Here is a quote from a former student who recognized this attribute: "I really have appreciated how 'right there' it always has seemed you are. I very much notice and appreciate all your speedy feedback, your comments, and your understanding to our personal lives. It would be hard online to give that feeling. It is this dialogue that makes me feel comfortable to email you. Thank you. Paul McGuire."

The typical responses to the tips that follow are exclamations such as:

"I wish someone would have shown me this a long time ago."
"Do you know how much time this will save me?"
"This is great! How did you learn this, or think this up?"

HANDLING EMAIL MORE EFFICIENTLY

Get a Separate Email Address for Online Teaching Work

The first piece of advice is to get a separate email address for online teaching. Most Internet Service Providers (ISPs) offer their subscribers more than one email address with an account. Use one of these unused-but-free email addresses from the local ISP that provides your Internet service. The drawback to an ISP email account, especially if the provider is a small local company, is that it can often only be accessed from the main home computer on which it is set up. Those who have good technical abilities can figure out how to access it on multiple computers, but it can be a challenge to set this up correctly.

Instructors who regularly use more than one computer or who travel frequently would benefit from a free web-based email account. These email programs can be accessed from any Internet-capable computer. Some examples are Hotmail and Yahoo Mail. One drawback is that these free accounts often receive a lot of SPAM or unsolicited emails. However, one advantage is that the email address is more universally recognized and therefore is generally easier to communicate to others.

Why Get a Separate Account?

There are several reasons to get a separate email address for online teaching. First, it will be less likely to get overloaded. Many email accounts have storage limitations. If personal and teaching emails are combined into one account, it is easier to reach that overload limit. For example, if Aunt June sends pictures that have not been resized and compressed or if the online students begin sending their projects via email attachment, it is likely that the storage limit will be reached. This will cause all further emails to "bounce-back" or be returned to the sender until email storage space is reopened by deleting stored emails. It can be disastrous to have emails bouncing-back since the online instructor is not even aware that messages from students have been rejected.

A separate email account also eliminates the possibility that other members of the household will open or even delete course emails. Once a message has been opened it usually changes from boldfaced type to regular type. If someone else in the house opened a course email by mistake, it would be very easy to overlook this now nonboldfaced message in the Inbox.

Email Folders

Most email programs allow the creation of new folders to hold received mail. Figure 6.1 shows email storage folders created to hold messages from each course module.

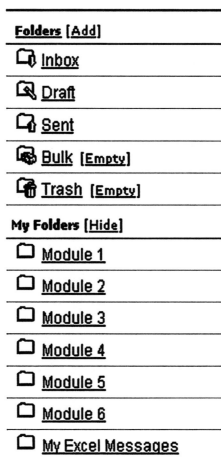

Figure 6.1. Email Storage Folders for Course Modules

With separate folders and good subject lines, discussed in a moment, it is easy to quickly sort mail and then store it so that it can be readily located for future reference.

Filters

In figure 6.2, it is apparent that any subject line containing the symbols #!# will be sorted into a folder for a particular course, in this case Reading. Students in the course have been asked to begin their subject lines with the symbol pattern #!#.

Since it is unlikely that a SPAM email will have this arrangement of symbols, when an email does have this subject-line pattern, it is most likely from a student in the course. The filter will automatically sort these emails into a designated folder. This is very handy if the instructor is teaching more than one course at a time. Students can be asked to use a variety of letters, symbols, or even simple word combinations so that email from each course goes into a separate folder. The instructor must remember then to check each folder since new emails will NOT be delivered to the inbox.

Subject Lines

The filter method taught above requires that students use a simple signal in their subject line so that email will be sorted into the appropriate folder. Stu-

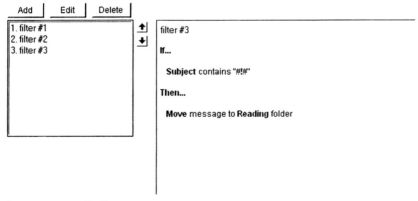

Figure 6.2.   Email Filters

dents can also be instructed to put other information in their subject lines to help the instructor deal with emails even more efficiently. The instructions should let students know to be as explicit as possible and include:

1. who the sender is,
2. the course they are taking with the instructor
3. the urgency of their message
4. something to indicate the topic of the email.

That sounds like a lot but it doesn't have to be. Students can use their first name/last initial or last name/first initial and one word of the course title or part of the course number. The word Help or Urgent can be added if the message needs to be answered quickly. Likewise, a student could put Not Urgent in a subject line for a message that does not require an immediate response. It helps to include this information on the course pages wherever appropriate. In the following example, the students have been directed to include the symbol "!" in the subject line, followed by their last name, then the current module number and a word indicating which assignment this email contains. This explicit subject line is easy for students to follow. Students can copy/paste the sample subject line from the course webpage and replace the term *Last-Name* with their own last name.

Please use this subject line when sending the email:
    EXAMPLE: #!# LastName.Mod1.Progression

STORING ASSIGNMENTS

Creating Folders for Assignments

Another tip for getting organized also uses folders. In this case the folders are for storing student assignments. These assignments might be stored on the hard drive of the computer, on a network drive, or on storage media such as a USB memory stick or a Zip drive cartridge. It is a good idea to have the assignments stored on two different places as a back up. Wherever the assignments are stored, folders are created to make storage and retrieval easier to manage.

In the following example, a folder is created for each week or module of the course. All assignments for the week are stored in the appropriate folder. Figures 6.3 and 6.4 are of a folder system for course 6661. There are four cohort groups in the current course. Each cohort group has its own folder and inside that folder is a folder for each week or module. The shot on the left shows the four cohort group folders and the shot on the right shows the folders inside the T70 cohort group folder.

Student assignments are saved into the proper folder when downloaded and are therefore easy to retrieve.

In figures 6.3 and 6.4, notice that there is a folder named "Correct Me I'm Late." The author created this folder to hold any late assignments until they are corrected. If late assignments are placed into the regular weekly folder, it is easy to forget to grade them since other assignments in that folder have presumably been graded. No matter what late policy an instructor has, there will always be instances of late assignments due to illness, emergency, or other understandable and unforeseen circumstances. Filing these late assignments in a special folder serves as a reminder to get them graded. After grading, the late assignment is moved into the appropriate weekly folder and deleted from the Correct Me I'm Late folder.

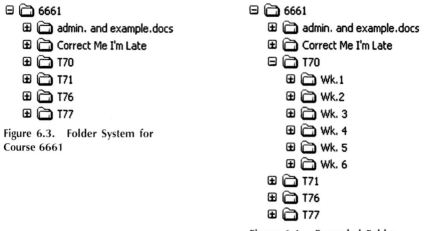

Figure 6.3. Folder System for Course 6661

Figure 6.4. Expanded Folder System for Course 6661

Personalize the Folder System

Both the email and the assignment storage folder systems work well for the author but it will be up to each individual to personalize his or her own storage system. One advantage of the systems described earlier is that copying the files after the course ends is quite easy. After a course ends it is a good idea to copy all the files to CD-ROM or other storage media for archival storage. It is rare that files from a previous course need to be retrieved, but it is possible to have a past student challenge his or her final grade. Some institutions require that records be kept for a certain length of time. Either way, it is just a good idea to archive files. Then the files can be deleted from the hard drive or network drive to free up storage space.

File-Naming Protocols

Just as students can be taught an email subject-line protocol they also can be expected to follow a file-naming protocol. This will make download and storage easier for the instructor and will ensure that the proper student gets the score for the assignment. Despite the fact that the author has teachers as students, no-name papers are as common in the online realm as they were while teaching eighth grade in the public schools. If the student's last name is part of the file name, it is much easier to identify no-name papers. Of course it also helps to expect papers to be properly headed with name, date, and the like, but the instructor still has to open each document to see the name on the assignment. Also, unique file names make it much harder to accidentally overwrite a file. If two people send in an assignment called SlideShow1 and they are to be saved in the same folder, the second project saved with that file title will overwrite, or replace, the first project. That means the first person's project is now gone from the computer's hard drive. Had these assignments arrived with names MAquiSlideShow and CwhiteSlideShow, there would be no possibility the instructor would have one file overwrite the other.

To make file naming easier, it is a good idea to give students a precise pattern to follow, along with an example. In the following example, notice that students are shown the pattern and then there is an explanation showing how to use the protocol. It is surprising how many projects and papers have been turned in by the student named LastName. :-)

ASSIGNMENT: Experiment with the Filters and create two filtered pictures. Upload them to your online photo storage site. Please also upload the originals for comparison purposes. Title the filtered picture files as follows:

LastName.Mod4.Filters.NameofFilter.jpg

So my photo, to which I have applied the Radial Blur filter, would be labeled as follows:

Lehmann.Mod4.Filters.RadialBlur.jpg

In the description area of the online photo album, please explain why you chose to use this filter.

Naming Protocols Are a Convenience

The online instructor needs to remember that file-naming and subject-line protocols are a nicety the students do to make our job easier. Chastising a student for forgetting one of these patterns would not be in order. A gentle reminder or an all-class message thanking specific individuals for doing this correctly should do the trick. And remember to be a good role model when writing instructor-initiated email subject lines.

Postgrading File-Naming Tip

One final tip about naming files: After a file has been graded, it is very handy to do a File/Save As and add something to the file name as a reminder that this paper or project has been graded. For example, after grading an assignment named M7ALewis the word "graded" could be added to the file name. The graded file would then be M7ALewisGRADED. This provides an at-a-glance reminder to the instructor which assignments have been graded and which have not. This can be a real time-saver if a grading session is unexpectedly interrupted.

MAIL MERGE

Another time-saver used by the author is to mail merge comments about assignments into a prewritten Word document. Very often when comments about an assignment are returned to the student, there are also some all-class announcements to be made. The specific comments to each person and their score are woven into the general comments everyone needs to hear. This forms a personalized message with all the appropriate information very quickly. Once the information has been merged it can be copy/pasted into an email, or it can be merged directly into an email message.

ONLINE TOOLS

Surveys

One very handy tool for gathering background information that will facilitate the formation of small groups and be helpful when troubleshooting is to gather data through a precourse survey. Some courseware systems have a quiz/survey feature the instructor can utilize for this. There are also online survey sites. An alternative to an electronic survey would be to formulate a survey as a word-processed document to be sent and returned via email attachment.

Some good items to include on the survey besides the basic demographics would be technical data. Knowing whether a student regularly uses a Macintosh computer or a windows-based PC, for example, can speed up troubleshooting dramatically. Also, having on hand some information about the general processor speed of the student's computer most regularly used for the course and his or her Internet connection speed can be helpful. Sometimes slow computer or connection speeds can cause the student's computer to "time-out" or stop downloading if the process is taking too long.

Keep in mind that many people don't know their exact computer processor or connection speed. The survey can be formatted in more general terms depending on the instructor's suppositions about the technical knowledge level of the group. A group of people taking an online C++ programming course would generally be much more knowledgeable about their computer equipment than those taking a course on the basics of word-processing software.

Online Gradebook

In many courseware systems, there is an online gradebook offering students easy access to their current scores and grade-to-date. Every instructor should also have this grade information stored offline somewhere. This could be a print-out, an exported or downloaded copy of the current scores, or a paper/pencil copy of the grades. In rare instances, the online gradebook can be lost due to technical problems. No instructor wants to re-create a gradebook from scratch midway through a course.

Other reasons to have easy access to an offline copy of the grades include being able to quickly answer student questions when they email or phone with a question and the ability for the instructor to work offline and away from the computer. If this offline copy of the grades is in an electronic form such as a downloaded copy of the gradebook or an Excel spreadsheet, the grades can become part of the archived records of the class mentioned earlier in the chapter.

Course Calendar

Use of a course calendar can be very helpful in eliminating email from students asking when assignments are due or when the course ends. Along with a course calendar, it is helpful to label each week's discussion or assignment pages with the dates for that week. This is a quick visual reminder to students about when the work must be completed. Any questions that students can answer for themselves eliminates one email that must be opened, answered, and sent.

COMMUNICATION TIMES

Efficiency can also be gained by setting up regular communication times. This includes setting at least one time per day for answering email. Responding to students' emails promptly will reduce anxiety on their part and will ultimately lessen the instructor's load because there will generally be fewer emails to answer in the long run if they are responded to promptly. Another type of regular communication is to hold online office hours at certain times each week. This can be done via chat or instant-messaging software. If students know that the instructor can be contacted in real time one or two times per week, this may cut down on the email load. The advantage of online office hours is that the instructor can be accomplishing other tasks until a student logs into the chat or instant-messaging (IM) system. Usually the entrance of someone into chat or IM is accompanied by a sound announcing an arrival. The disadvantage of online office hours is that the instructor needs to be faithful about being online at those times. Remember that any synchronous communications such as chat can be a challenge to schedule if participants in the course are geographically diverse.

TRIAL AND ERROR

All of the tips shared in this chapter were learned through trial and error by the author. Each reader now has a jumpstart on efficiency but each idea will need to be tweaked until the best efficiency patterns are found.

7

The Crucial First Week

GETTING STARTED IN AN ONLINE COURSE

The most crucial time for maintaining student enrollment in a course is just before and through the first week. Students who are unsure of themselves as online learners and/or who are squeamish about this new environment will back out of a course in the first few days. Any investment of money that has already been made can usually be recouped and their investment of time and energy is minimal. This makes it easy for them to say, "I'm going to cut my losses and run now." Most of the time unfortunately, people drop a class they would have enjoyed and benefited from had there been some encouragement to stick it out.

Once students make connections with peers and the investment of both time and money has grown, students are less likely to drop out. After that first week, some people who drop out of a class are self-selecting themselves as not fit for the online environment. They have come to realize they do not have the attributes of good online learners. One other thing to keep in mind is that there will always be life circumstances that cause students to drop out throughout a class. The online instructor cannot prevent all dropouts; however, they can prevent those who are dropping out because of fear.

COMMUNICATION IS THE KEY

Maintaining enrollment isn't even the most important consideration when thinking about this crucial early period. Getting everyone off to a great start is the most important task of the online instructor. So what can the online instructor do to help maintain full enrollment in a class and get everyone off to a great start? The first thing is to communicate; the second thing is to communicate; and the third thing is to communicate. Helping learners new to the online environment get settled in and off to a great start requires lots of instructor communication. Later in the class, the instructor can begin to ease his or her voice out of discussions, letting the learners take over the communication reins. Early on the teacher carries most of the communication bundle.

Anxiety Attacks

My observation, based on experiences with hundreds of online learners, is that most first-time online learners are extremely nervous prior to a class. Nervous to the point of anxiety attacks! Why so anxious? Unfamiliarity! As of June 2000, "less than one percent of the U.S. population has taken an online course, according to an estimate by market research company IDC" (Batista, 2000). Most people have no idea what to expect. Everyone has been to school. They understand how the process works in a face-to-face classroom environment. Even if someone is unsure about what to expect from a particular face-to-face course, they at least have some general idea how face-to-face classes operate.

In the online world nothing is familiar. There is no classroom. They won't see their instructor or their fellow students. They aren't even sure how they will turn in assignments. The student doesn't even need to buy a new binder to clutch as a security blanket. So the first job of the instructor is to reach out to these very anxious students and begin to reassure them. Earlier chapters of the book discussed how to make warm, human connections with others online. During this crucial precourse period is when these human connections are being formed between the instructor and individual students. The question is, how does the online instructor alleviate this anxiety in a course that has not even begun?

Precourse Communications

Start with an email! Prior to the start of class, most institutions send the instructor a roster of students, with student email addresses. The email addresses are important. If the institution doesn't send them, see if there is a way to get them so that communications can get started. As early as possible, send all students an introductory email message that includes a brief instructor introduction and an invitation to respond with any questions or concerns. It is recommended that this first message be kept short. Here is an example of an introductory message:

My name is Kay Lehmann, and I am the online instructor for our online course that begins soon. I am looking forward to getting to know more about you.

Before our course officially begins on Monday, there is one additional thing you can do to get ready. Check your computer's antivirus software. Make sure that it is both updating itself regularly AND scanning your computer regularly. It needs to do both of those things to protect your computer. The last thing that you want to have happen is to get a computer virus that ruins your hard drive. I don't want that to happen to you either! Or to me for that matter! ☺

I will be in touch again over the weekend with some instructions and information on how to find course materials and what to expect in the class. If you have any questions or concerns at any time, please feel free to contact me at this email address. I am here to help!

This contact will generate several emails from grateful students who will confess their anxiety level was ultrahigh and that this simple contact has reassured them. Guaranteed!

Continue to Be Proactive

This first email is just one way to be proactive when teaching online. Another way is to send quick, informative emails, or post a FAQ page with information about how things work in the online course. Joan Vandervelde, an online learning expert, calls these "Administrivia." These messages include all the little things that would be covered in an orientation and/or in the first few days of a face-to-face course. Making this information available just in time is another way to reduce student anxiety.

For the first few weeks of a course, many students will continue to be highly anxious whenever they don't know how to proceed; yet they are reticent to contact the instructor with what they feel might be a "dumb question." Anticipating some of those questions and providing the answers before the questions are even asked is highly reassuring. These can be sent throughout the first week or two so as not to overwhelm the learners.

Another proactive step is to double-check all the links in the course site. The instructor should do this before every new module, but it is especially important in the first week or two. Again, running into a bad link for a required reading can make the new online learner highly anxious since he or she has no idea how to proceed from that point.

The day before the class begins, plan to send another welcome message with more details, including how to log into the course site and how to proceed once the student has logged in. If the institution or entity has an orientation program, this step may not be necessary. One sign that an all-class message should be sent is if more than one person has asked the question via email. If two or more people have a question and are willing to email it to the instructor, it is very likely that many more people have the same question and are still not comfortable contacting the instructor with what they think is a dumb question.

There Are No Dumb Questions

No question is a dumb question if it is causing anxiety to the student. Instructors will receive questions that make their eyebrows rise and their heads shake but this disbelief should never be communicated to the student. Ever! If an instructor answers curtly or suggests in any way that this was a dumb question, it will shut down communication with that student. Then, when a more important question about the course comes up, the student will be unwilling to contact the instructor and his or her assignments or participation will suffer because he or she didn't know how to proceed.

Students willing to contact the instructor with questions should be praised. This is part of the process of making connections. Students who begin to feel comfortable asking questions will then encourage others to ask questions. Better yet, many will begin to feel comfortable enough to answer questions posed by others. That empowerment of the learners is a major goal of the online instructor. As much time as it takes to be highly communicative and proactive early in the course, it will pay dividends later in the course when students are empowered to conduct their learning without as much instructor attention. Here are a couple of ways to let students know that questions are welcomed and encouraged:

"Great question, I am so glad you asked this!"
    "I am so glad you brought this up. I am sure others are wondering the same thing."
    "Thanks for asking a terrific question!"

There will be more information about how to empower students in chapter 8.

GETTING PEER–PEER CONTACTS STARTED

Not only do students need to be comfortable with instructor–student communications, it is important in most online courses to encourage peer interactions. Many students at first find this awkward since the visual aspect of the face-to-face connection is missing. For some reason, not being able to see the faces of others really impedes some online learners. Most get over this quickly when peer communications begin to blossom. How can the instructor encourage that blossoming?

Introductory Activity

Provide students with an introductory activity that encourages them to post something about themselves personally and professionally. The instructor should post his or her own response first as a model for others. The activity needs to be specific enough to encourage students to post more than name, rank, and serial number, as it were. The more substantive the information that learners post about themselves, the more connections that will be made with others. Students sometimes need to be encouraged to say a little more about themselves. Here is an instructor posting that encourages the student to flesh out their introduction and offers some suggestions of what to include:

Glad you joined us, Angie! Tell us what fun things you are doing this summer. Do you have any hobbies? Are you planning to read any good books? Do you share your life with friends, family, or pets? The more we know about each other, the more connections we can make to help us enjoy this course together. Thanks for introducing yourself!

If the instructor had just posted, "Tell us more about yourself," the student may have floundered, or even been somewhat insulted that his or her posting wasn't good enough. Remember that text-only messages can come across as cold or terse, and it is possible that a short declarative statement like "Tell us more about yourself" could be more harmful than helpful in encouraging communication.

It is important that the instructor respond to every one of the personal introduction postings. This reassures the individual student, validates his or her posting, and provides the instructor an opportunity to model some discussion techniques for everyone's benefit. In all other discussions in the course, the instructor should not respond to every posting. This will subdue peer interaction, as everyone will be looking to the instructor for "the answer." The instructor needs to be visible in the discussions by posting some thoughts each day but the majority of the discussion should occur peer to peer. As the course continues and peers become more adept at responding well, the instructor can continue to reduce his or her visibility in the discussion. The teacher's presence should always be felt, but it can fade somewhat as the course matures.

Student Lounge

Some type of open forum should be made available for students to discuss items outside the scope of the course. This same forum, called the Student Lounge for the purposes of this book, can be used for the introduction activity but students should be encouraged to continue to use it after the introductory period ends. This same area could also be a place in which to ask questions. Some instructors prefer to have one forum for casual conversations and another specifically devoted to questions. Posting questions for everyone to see encourages peers to offer answers. It also allows others who may have the same, albeit unasked, question to find out the answer without sending a private instructor email.

Signatures

Students should be encouraged to sign postings and emails with their full name and location. This is especially helpful when the group is geographically diverse. The instructor can model this for students and then celebrate those who follow the pattern. The same holds true for signing email messages; the instructor should model good signature lines in all instructor–student email communications and should encourage students to do the same.

FIRST WEEK TIME COMMITMENT

Every instructor should allow extra time in his or her schedule for answering emails and student postings during the first week of a course. Encouraging student communication is an important goal and promptly answering the first flurry of anxious emails and postings will go a long way toward meeting that goal.

Students new to online learning should have an easy workload during the first week. Assignments and readings should be kept purposely light to encourage the peer–peer interactions in the introductions. The first assignments should be manageable, even easy, so that each student feels successful at the end of the first week. Many new online learners are easily overwhelmed, especially if the introductory discussion becomes lengthy or if for some reason they login late that first week. Late arrivals can happen for a variety of reasons including technical problems. These latecomers are almost always stressed because of their late start. Extra attention must be paid until the latecomers are well underway.

CONFIDENCE BUILDING

As can be seen from many of the tips in this chapter, much of the first week is spent building the confidence of the learners. Confidence building doesn't end after that first week. In chapter 5, some ways to build student confidence through communication were explored. In the next chapter, assessment of student's work is discussed. It may seem like assessment would not fall under the confidence-building banner, but it very much does. Good assessment techniques will help students develop skills while improving their self-esteem.

8

Assessment in the Online Environment

Assessment of student work is more than grading a paper and assigning a score. In the online classroom, assessment is a very important part of the communication process that helps students build their skills and knowledge base and more importantly aids their personal/professional growth. When assessment is done well it can guide students to find their own answers, improve their performance, and fix their mistakes. Creating a high-quality assessment system begins before the course starts.

FORMATIVE AND SUMMATIVE ASSESSMENT

In educational terms there are two types of assessment, formative and summative. Formative assessment guides the student in fixing his or her own mistakes and helps the student grow as he or she progresses through the course. In an online course, this would include all instructor commentary about assignments, participation, and any other type of student work. Summative assessment is a more holistic look at the student's work in the course and is usually communicated as a letter grade at the end of the course. In terms of helping learners grow and develop, the more important assessment type is formative. The remainder of this chapter will be concerned with various types of formative assessment.

BEGINNING AT THE BEGINNING WITH ASSESSMENT

The instructor, or sometimes the institution/entity, will define in advance how the course will be graded. This is usually contained in a syllabus or course outline and should include the grading scale, objectives to be met/standards to be assessed, expectations for student work in all parts of the course, and rubrics. Rubrics guide students as they work and are used for instructor grading. For the most part, the grading scale or grading system will be defined by the institution/entity so no further discussion of that will take place.

Objectives and/or Standards

Objectives and or standards are the measures by which student learning will be judged. This colloquialism states the importance of predetermining outcomes succinctly: "How will you know when you get there if you don't know where you are going?" Experienced teachers understand the importance of defining in advance how student success will be measured in the course.

These definitions may be standards, preset by an agency such as a credentialing commission, in which case the student will show mastery of the standards through his or her coursework. Some examples of standards are shown here:

The standards below were set by the California Commission on Teacher Credentialing and are part of the Level II Professional Proficiency Standards to earn the Level II CLEAR credential. This is just a portion of the standards that must be met to earn this teacher credential.

2.2   Each candidate interacts and collaborates with others using computer-based collaborative tools.

2.7   Each candidate uses technology in lessons to increase each student's ability to plan, locate, evaluate, select and use information to solve problems and draw conclusions.

2.11   Each candidate contributes to site-based planning or local decision-making regarding the use of technology and acquisition of technological resources.

Curricular objectives are a common type of definition. Objectives state how the teacher will know when the student has succeeded.

These objectives are from a variety of teacher professional development courses:

Identify the resources needed to complete the planned digital imaging project

Correctly perform a data sort with and without a header row using more than one criteria

Discuss how cooperative learning techniques should be adapted and used when working with learners with special needs

Whether the outcomes are stated as standards, objectives, or some other method, they should be clearly outlined in advance and should be the foundation of the assignments/projects in the course. A rubric should then be created that states the criteria on which the assignment or project will be graded and the value placed on each of the criteria.

Rubrics

A well-written rubric guides the student to create a high-quality project that meets the outcomes to be assessed and it helps the instructor to quickly and objectively grade student projects. A rubric needs to state each criteria being assessed as well as the quality levels and associated point values for each criteria. An example of a rubric is shown in table 8.1.

The rubric should be provided to the student before the assignment/ project begins. This allows him or her to competently meet all the criteria to successfully complete the project. A great resource to help teachers build rubrics is Rubistar (http://rubistar.4teachers.org/). This online site is a wonderful resource for criteria and performance level definitions.

Communicating Expectations

Before assessing any work, the instructor should communicate his or her expectations to students. In particular the instructor should relate his or her expectations for student participation and the consequences for turning in late work. Putting these expectations in the syllabus is a good plan. Keep in mind that some students never read the syllabus. Stating the expectations in announcements or postings is another good way to reach everyone. It is also a good idea to revisit expectations via all-class emails or forum postings as problems crop up, or even better, before they crop up.

Table 8.1. Sample Rubric for Electronic Gradebook Assignment

Element	Points	Criteria for Full Credit	Criteria for Partial Credit
Output lists points possible as well as points earned	1	Points possible and points earned are shown so that a reader can compare the two.	No partial credit available.
Student is anonymous but can self-identify	2	Student's name is not listed but some method is used that allows the student to identify their own scores and a short explanation of the method for creating an anonymous identifier is included.	For 1 pt. Explanation does not explain the method for creating the anonymous identifier or it is unclear how the student will be able to identify their own scores.
Cumulative final grade included	1	Grade to date is shown as a letter grade or percentage score.	No partial credit available.
Explanation of cost/ease of use/features	2	Explanation of the benefits/drawbacks of this tool and why it was chosen for use over other tools is present.	For 1 pt. Explanation does not adequately address why this tool was chosen or does not include inform- ation on cost, ease of use. or features.
Explanation of uses for assessment and communication	4	Explanation of how this tool will improve communication about assessment to students and parents.	For 2 pts. Explanation fails to show that communication will be improved, or fails to address either student or parent communication.
TOTAL	10		

ASSESSING PARTICIPATION

What is participation? In the face-to-face environment, many teachers ex-pect students to participate in class discussions and to do cooperative group projects. The online environment is no different. Most online courses that have an instructor also have a peer group with whom each student should communicate. If the course has a peer–peer aspect, there are usually expectations for participation in discussions or projects. How to define participation is the challenge.

Discussion Participation

At a minimum, most instructors expect each student to post an original response to every discussion question and respond substantively to the postings of others. Some instructors want the original response posted by mid-week; others don't care when it is posted as long as it occurs during the week. The harder point to assess is whether the responses to others are substantive. A colleague at Walden University, Ossil Macavinta, developed a system that works well (personal communication, 2003). Here are the categories Ossil developed to assess the quality of discussion responses:

- Referred to course materials
- Referred to colleagues' comments
- Provided constructive feedback
- Enhanced the quality of the discussion
- Met minimum requirements of the discussion question
- Posted response by the due date

The most important thing about assessing discussion participation is that the instructor comments and grading lead to improvement in future weeks. Students may need to be shown examples of postings that are substantive. It is important to point out what the student is doing right as well as where improvement is needed. This is always true of assessment.

The Sandwich Method

An astute principal once shared that the best way to begin a parent–teacher conference was for the teacher to say something nice about the child. Every parent wants to hear something good about his or her child and it softens the bad news the teacher may need to impart when parents have already heard something positive. This same method, known as the sandwich method, works well when providing assessment comments about discussions, assignments, or anything else.

Begin the assessment comments by mentioning something good in the work. This is the first layer of bread in the sandwich. Then state the things that need improvement. This is the meat or filling in the sandwich. End with another positive comment. That is the top piece of bread in the sandwich. This method really works! Here is a comment from a former student comparing the author's assessment method with another online instructor:

"My other class is over now and I got a perfect score but it doesn't feel as good as getting a high score in your class. Please remind teachers that when they don't have face-to-face contact they ought to be very specific and detailed in their feedback, as you were. In this class it seemed as though there were a boilerplate evaluation, 'Dear _____, I have just reviewed your _____ assignment. You did an outstanding job and have been awarded 50 points.' I don't know what was outstanding and what needed work" (Joan Chu, personal communication, 2003).

TO QUIZ OR NOT TO QUIZ

Depending on the type of course, assignments and participation scoring may form the bulk of grading to be done by the instructor. Some online courses use online self-grading exams, relieving the instructor of the burden of grading tests. However, unless the material to be learned is highly fact-based, exams are not a very effective assessment method. They are also the least secure assessment method in the online environment. In other words, it is much easier to cheat on an online quiz than it is to cheat on a well-designed assignment. It is also hard to design an online quiz or test that accurately assesses highly complex knowledge or procedures. For these reasons, quizzes should be used as checkpoints. For the most part, quizzes should not form the bulk of the points in an online instructor-led course.

CHEATING

Many people ask, "How do you know online students you've never met really write the papers they submit?" The answer to that question is another question, "How does any teacher know any student really writes the paper he or she submits?" Well-designed assignments and discussion questions require individualized responses. It doesn't take an instructor long to learn the style and tone of each student, whether it is in the face-to-face environment or the online world. Any deviation from that "voice" is obvious to the astute instructor. A response that is too generalized or doesn't really fit the assignment criteria is cause for concern. Yet that concern has to be very carefully voiced in the online environment because of the limitations of text-based communications that have already been discussed. In fact, concern that cheating has occurred is the perfect time to use a nineteenth-century technology. Reach for the telephone and call the student. A discussion of integrity and ethics is a time when hearing voice inflections may be highly beneficial on both sides.

If plagiarism is suspected, it is easy to check out this suspicion. The instructor should copy a long passage from the paper or assignment that includes some unique phrasing. Paste that passage, inside quotation marks, into any search engine. The quotation marks will ensure that the search engine looks for the entire passage, not the individual words in the selection. If the search engine gets a match, the instructor can read the online article to determine if plagiarism has really occurred. It is a good idea to run several phrases from the suspect paper through the search engine before making a determination that cheating has occurred. Online services such as TurnItIn (http://www.turnitin.com/), are designed to catch plagiarized papers and can be very helpful, but they are expensive. The search engine trick will usually catch any problem by showing the true source of the material.

The most important thing to remember is that a well-designed assignment that calls for an individualized response will cut down on cheating. A side benefit is that it will make the instructor's life more interesting, since every assignment will be a bit different. Here are examples of assignment directions for comparison. The first is a poorly designed assignment statement. The second is a much better assignment. Judge for yourself which would be the more difficult on which to cheat.

1. Write a 2 page paper explaining France's Bastille Day holiday and why it is important.
2. Compare and contrast the United States's Fourth of July holiday with the French holiday called Bastille Day.

ASSESSING ASSIGNMENTS

Students who are given clear expectations and well-written assignment objectives and who possess the rubric that will be used to grade the assignment should produce a high-quality product. Assigning a letter or numerical score to those high-quality products is generally easy. That leaves the instructor free to comment on the content of the assignment, to ask thought-provoking questions, and offer suggestions for extending the student's learning.

Unfortunately, a lot of instructors seem to feel that assigning the letter or numerical grade is all that is needed. Students in the online classroom, perhaps more so than in the face-to-face classroom, crave feedback about their work. Online students are isolated in their homes, schools, or offices with no teacher handy to whom questions can be addressed. As instructors this is our opportunity to help them extend their learning. Students need substantive feedback and that feedback needs to occur in a timely manner.

For changes in practice or thinking to occur, feedback needs to follow the completion of an assignment as quickly as possible. Here is a quote from a student who is grateful for timely feedback about her participation in a new online course:

"Your comments about the discussions were very helpful. I like to know how things are going and what is expected of me before new assignments. One thing that I have found somewhat difficult with an online course is not knowing if I'm doing the things expected of me. I have read the criteria of the discussions. Your comments make those clearer. Thanks again" (Kathy Bishop, personal communication, 2003).

Offering personalized, timely feedback often brings another plus. It opens the door to more communication opportunities with the student. When students feel they can talk openly with the instructor it is easier to smooth over temporary rough spots and perhaps prevent the underground rumble discussed in chapter 5. Here is a comment from a student that shows the benefit of good quality feedback:

"Thank you for the feedback. I have been very anxious to hear back from you because like you have stated, some of us have been out of school for a long time. This is a new experience and you know being out of your comfort zone takes a while to adjust" (Pam Fields, personal communication, 2003).

ALTERNATIVES TO INSTRUCTOR FEEDBACK

Student Self-Evaluation

One way to lessen the burden of providing feedback to students and encourage empowerment at the same time is to occasionally have students self-assess their work. This can be done using a rubric and/or a reflective journal entry. The student self-assessment can form part of the assignment grade along with instructor scoring, or this could be an assignment that is not scored at all except to note that it was completed.

Peer Evaluations

Another method of assessment is peer–peer evaluation. This can be done through informal comments in the discussion forum or in a more formalized manner using a rubric and commentary. When done informally in a discussion thread, students will usually post their assignment as an attachment for all to see. Colleagues are then encouraged to offer substantial comments. If done too early in a class, the peer–peer communication may be too sugary, without offering anything that could remotely be seen as a negative or critical comment. It is a good idea to wait to try this until the group shows they are able to have discussions that include disagreeing with a point made by someone. Disagreement, done correctly, is healthy for a discussion. Evaluating peer assignments with constructive criticism requires the ability to point out errors. This is a form of disagreeing with someone. When informal peer commentary is used, it is critical that the instructor make sure everyone receives some comments on the posted assignment. If peers don't comment on the assignment within one to two days, the instructor should comment on the assignment and include a message that encourages peers to join in the dialogue.

More formal peer–peer assessments involve each student determining all or part of a score for his or her colleague. These should not be attempted until after the small groups have been allowed to gel. Chapter 9 is devoted to setting up, using, and monitoring peer groups in online classes including peer feedback and assessment.

9

Cooperative Learning Online

WHY DO GROUPS?

Anyone who has ever worked on a small group project knows sometimes this is a frustrating experience. A common complaint is that one person does most of the work and/or there is one person who does almost nothing. Another lament often heard is that one person has taken over and is bossing the rest of the group. The question begging to be asked is, "If there are so many potential headaches inherent in small group work, why bother doing them?"

CREATING CONNECTIONS IN THE ONLINE WORLD

Small groups promote an increased level of communications and involvement that might not otherwise occur in an online course. Much of this book has discussed the importance of creating connections between instructor and students. And while that is important, many of the truly lasting connections that will occur in an online course are inside the peer group. These are, after all, colleagues with similarity in age, work, or some other interest that brought each person into a particular course or program. Some peers will connect with each other in an online course no matter what the instructor does, but with a bit of facilitation many more connections will be made before the course is over—connections like the ones discussed here by a student named Stephanie who was grateful to Valerie, another student in the class, for posting a potential job opening.

"Hi, Valerie. It's posts like yours that remind me of how connected an online community of learners can be. Many times when I tell people that I'm enrolled in a Master's degree program taught entirely online, most of them immediately think that learners are isolated and alone. After one week of meeting new colleagues and renewing acquaintances with those from previous classes, I feel more connected in this environment than I ever did in all of my on-ground courses" (Stephanie Watts, personal communication, 2002).

JUST LET THEM PICK THEIR PARTNERS?

There are two possible options for setting up peer groups in a course. One is to have the instructor assign groups. The other is to let people in the course seek out partners from among the members of the group. This has the potential to leave people out, just as it would in the face-to-face environment. The advantage of self-selected groups is that people who have already bonded with classmates can choose to work together. They already feel comfortable and share common interests with those whom they self-select.

Self-Selecting Groups

Online teachers who choose to let students self-select groups need to be very clear up front about group size. When the instructor forms the groups, the size is easy to control. When students begin contacting one another about forming a small group, there is often a tumbleweed effect. For example, Josey contacted Su about working together in a group. Su said she contacted June who will get back to Su as soon as William answers the email June sent to him. Pretty soon what was supposed to be a group of two or three will be four or five strong because no one wants to hurt anyone else's feelings by saying, "I decided to join a different group after I emailed an invitation to you."

On the flip side, there needs to be a mechanism for people who are completely left out of the groupings to contact the instructor and be placed in a group. This scenario is awkward and has the potential to be very painful for the student who is excluded, even if it was completely unintentional. Being left out is more likely to occur online because it is impossible to see the groups forming. In the face-to-face environment, the instructor can see who is on the periphery, in danger of being excluded, and can subtly correct this problem.

Instructor-Selected Groupings

A better option is to use information and observations to create instructor-selected groups. The information source might be a preclass questionnaire or the introductory postings. The advantage to instructor-created groups is that no one will be left out. The disadvantage is that the instructor has a limited amount of knowledge, especially if groups need to be formed early in the course, which can be used to create the groups.

An online instructor who will be using cooperative peer groups needs to first determine the purpose and functions of the groups. This will help in the selection process. For example, in a highly technical class it would be helpful to put students with lower technical skills/knowledge with students of higher ability. The higher-ability students can assist those with less knowledge while working on the project. Very likely they will continue in an unofficial mentoring role after the project is completed. Once a relationship is formed, groups usually communicate and help one another throughout the course.

If the purpose of the groups is to learn to work with some type of diversity such as job functions, then the instructor needs to put people from different job tracks or departments together. Prethinking the purpose and functions of the group process is critical.

The teacher then needs to gather information. As stated previously, this can be through questionnaires or surveys, via analysis of posted messages, or by looking for patterns. Questionnaires are very helpful in determining fact-based information such as job titles or things that can be accurately self-assessed. Posted messages can offer insights about temperament and characteristics. Students in online courses quickly develop patterns that can be observed by an alert instructor. Here is a comment from a member of a small group whose interests were well matched by the instructor:

"I really enjoyed this week because it was the first time I got to work closely with a small group of people. I met my group for the first time and we found that our interests and experiences complemented each other (probably encouraged by you!) You did a great job matching us up" (Kelly Sommers, personal communication, 2003).

The Power of Patterns

Noticing, for example, which students post messages the minute a new thread is opened versus those who post at the last minute offers insight into the working styles of the participants. Someone who posts at the first possible opportunity is very likely to be the type of person who wants to get right to work on a project and get it submitted early. Conversely, those who post at the last minute may choose to pull a last-minute all-nighter and get the project submitted just before the deadline. These two types of people do not make good groupmates. Neither is right or wrong; their working styles are just incompatible and conflict will inevitably result.

Communicating and Monitoring

It seems to help alleviate some of the anxiety that results from forming groups if the instructor is honest about the perils of group work. Encourage everyone from the beginning to keep the instructor informed. In fact, one way to stay informed is to be an unofficial member of every group. For example, if copies of group emails go to the teacher as well as all the students, the teacher can listen in, or lurk, on the group conversations. The teacher has to avoid the tendency to get involved or meddle in the group. There is a fine line between monitoring to be proactive and meddling in the group dynamics.

Another method of monitoring groups is to have a designated time at which all groups report progress to the instructor. Groups that have been procrastinating about a large-scale project will respond to this reporting deadline by getting down to business. This interim report also lets the instructor see if the work seems to be divided fairly. Whatever monitoring methods are used, it is important that the online teacher be aware of progress. It is counterproductive to have someone email and say, "The group hasn't done anything. I want out!" just before the project is due.

Even with marvelous efforts at carefully forming groups and monitoring them, every instructor will eventually hear from someone who does want to switch groups. Sometimes there is a strong and rational reason to say yes to a switch. However, this is awkward because the result will disrupt two groups, not one. The group the student is leaving and the group being joined will both be temporarily out of balance. Making the switch in a way that does not leave hurt feelings is a communications challenge for any instructor and should not be done lightly.

Here is an example of one message used by the author to let a group know that a member will be leaving:

"Hello Plum group members! I am very sorry to inform you that I am going to have to relieve you of a groupmate. I had an error in my records and had Shelly assigned to two different groups. Yikes! I've determined that Shelly needs to work with the other of the two groups to which I mistakenly assigned her. She and I only recently discovered this mistake. I am so sorry to do this, but I know that this is a strong group and you will be able to carry on without Shelly. Please accept my apologies."

When the instructor shoulders the onus, the integrity of the whole class isn't at risk. At worst, the small group will be angry with the instructor. If they were angry with the departing group member, that discontent could spread to other groups or throughout the class. No matter how this is done, though, it does cause ripples in the class and should not be done lightly.

Likewise no one should be allowed to work solo on a project when others are required to complete it in groups. It is a rare group that does not struggle to complete a project and many people would much prefer to just "do it myself." If the instructor allows one individual to do the project solo, discontent will result.

ASSESSING GROUP WORK

There are two aspects to assessing group work, product and process. The first, product, is the assessment of the final project produced by the group. The second is process. How well did the group communicate and cooperate? Was the workload equally shared? Both product and process should be a part of the final group grade.

Product

Scoring the product of a group is much like scoring a project from an individual. Using a rubric, a numeric or letter grade is determined. The instructor offers feedback on the project to everyone in the group. Other groups may also informally assess or comment on the product.

Process

Instructors should also grade the process used by the group to create their project. If points are only awarded for the product, then the group has no real reason to work together. One person could submit a project and everyone in the group would benefit whether they worked on it or not.

Therefore, it is important that the online instructor somehow assess the group process. The question becomes, how can this be done when the instructor never actually sees the groups in action? Monitoring the groups gives the instructor an indication before the assignment is submitted about how effectively the group process has gone. These observations can be combined with information from members of the group. One of the best ways to assess the group process is to have each individual in the group complete a journal entry about the experience. The journal question should be stated so that each person assesses their own work level as well as the work of their groupmates. Another way to assess the process is to ask each member of the group to score other members of the group with a rubric such as the one in table 9.1.

PEER–PEER REVIEW

One great function of small groups is peer review. In chapter 8, an informal method of peer assessment or peer review was discussed. This involved commentary on individual projects posted for the whole group to review. Here a more formalized type of peer assessment is the topic. Review by a peer is less threatening than assessment by an instructor. Peer feedback can be not only honest and forthright, it can be highly valuable. This is especially true when individuals with similar jobs or goals have been partnered. They can share experiences and knowledge with their partner.

One way to use peer feedback effectively is to have peers review/edit works in progress. By having peers compare a current project to a rubric, or by mutually editing papers, each individual gets a snapshot view of the project/paper before submitting it to the instructor for final grading. Be sure to allow plenty of time in the schedule when using peer review. It takes a while for this process to take place.

Table 9.1. Group Work and Participation Rubric

Score each of your teammates on the following criteria

Criteria	4 = Excellent	3 = Very Good	2 = Improving	1 = Needs Work	Points Earned
Attitude	Considered and validated all viewpoints in the group. Communications were friendly and encouraging.	Usually considered and validated all viewpoints in the group. Most communications were friendly and encouraging.	Occasionally considered and validated viewpoints of the group. Some communications were rude or dismissive.	Rarely considered viewpoints offered by others. Communications tended to be rude, dismissive, or negative.	
Participation	Always did their work without being reminded by others and encouraged others to complete their work.	Rarely needed reminders to complete work and often encouraged others to complete their work.	Often needed reminders to complete work and was not encouraging to others.	Needed lots of reminders to complete work.	
Work Share	Completed their fair share of the work and encouraged others to do a fair share.	Completed nearly their fair share of the work but pawned a little work off on others.	Completed less than their fair share of the work and left others to do more than their share.	Did not do a fair share of the work.	
Communication	Stayed in touch with members of the group, responding promptly to emails.	Occasionally left members waiting for information or a response.	Often left members waiting for information or a response.	Rarely responded in a timely fashion to others.	
Collaboration	Actively helped the group set goals and complete their tasks without taking over the group.	Usually helped the group set goals and complete their tasks.	With prompting helped the group set goals and complete their tasks.	Not helpful to the group when setting goals and completing their tasks.	

A timeline of the peer review process might look like this:

1. Paper or project is created.
2. Paper/project is sent to the peer.
3. The peer edits the paper/project.
4. Peer returns the item with comments to the original author.
5. The original author corrects the project/paper based on the comments.
6. And finally, the paper/project is submitted to the instructor.

CONNECTEDNESS

Many, many students have written to the author and said that while the group process was difficult in some way, they knew that they were better for having participated. Here are some comments about group connectedness that state it more eloquently:

"I've never done a group project with people I've never met before. This is an interesting experience for me in that regard. I'm also rather frustrated with the process as well . . . it would be easier for me to do this project individually instead of with a group.

With that said, I have enjoyed receiving my group's input and sharing ideas with them. We were very slow in starting to communicate with each other, and we definitely procrastinated getting started on the project. Once it got moving, though, progress was made quickly. I enjoyed making suggestions and seeing them implemented by others and implementing others' suggestions myself" (Jonathan Hoffman, personal communication, 2003).

"There is always something that can go wrong, and it is more difficult to solve it when all you have to communicate is an email address. They have the choice of answering or ignoring you. Overall the group project was fun; I enjoyed the interaction and the observation of other professionals" (Gloria Yniguez, personal communication, 2003).

10

Course Design Tips

This is a book about how to be a good online teacher, not a good online course designer. But here are a few course design and curriculum tips that can be helpful for the online instructor to know, even when the curriculum is predetermined by the institution or agency. Through instructions, announcements, or discussion postings, the instructor can make adjustments to the course that will make the students' experience more worthwhile.

DISCUSSION QUESTIONS

A well-written discussion question will engage every student in the course. People will be able to respond with a unique and insightful answer based on their own knowledge and experiences. Others will be compelled to respond to these unique answers with questions, commentary, and suggestions that take the discussion deeper. This can be an exhilarating experience for students and teacher alike.

A good discussion question does not have a yes or no answer. In fact, there should be no one right answer to the question because after it is posted every other answer will be the equivalent of "I agree." Boring! This is not a good discussion result in any educational environment.

When the Flaw Is Noted in Advance

What can the instructor do if it is clear in advance that a discussion question is flawed? If the online teacher has the authority to change the question, then it should be changed before the students ever see the question. If the facilitator does not have access to change the question, a request can be sent to someone in the sponsoring agency requesting a change. This often requires some lead time at the institution or agency. Notifying the institution should occur at the earliest moment that the flaw is spotted.

Dealing with a Flaw before the Discussion Begins

The instructor may spot the flaw but be unable to effect a change. If students have not begun answering the question yet, the instructor can post a reply to the original question that extends the original question or even replaces it. It is best not to tell the students that this is a "bad question" but instead alternative ways to answer it can be offered. Here is a flawed question that easily could have resulted in a chorus of "I agree." Notice the reply by the instructor urging students to a new direction without finding fault in the original question.

Original question from a course about classroom inclusion of students with special needs: "What types of duties do paraprofessionals have in your school?"

Instructor reply: "In most schools around the country, the duties of paraprofessionals are pretty much the same. Maria, Angela, and Charles have already mentioned some of the major duties and it is likely that those same duties will be echoed by the rest of you. Instead of continuing to list the same jobs over and over again, let's consider the following statement. Please respond whether you agree or disagree and support your opinion with reasons or examples. Statement: The work of a paraprofessional in the inclusive classroom is just as important as the work of the teacher.

You are encouraged to respond to the postings of others with questions, comments, and polite disagreement."

Dealing with a Flaw after the Discussion Has Begun

Many times, the instructor will not realize the question is flawed until the discussion is underway. Most good classroom teachers know how to refocus a discussion. The same techniques are used in the online environment, but because this is a new medium for most teachers, a short dialogue about how to refocus is included here.

If the discussion group is replying with a chorus of "I agree" to a flawed question, what can be done? The instructor can ask individuals to explain why they agree and/or ask them to give an example of why they believe this point to be true. Or a second question could be posed by the instructor accompanied by a statement such as, "It seems nearly everyone agrees with the position stated by Hal. Since that is the case, let's consider the following . . ." The new question or topic can then be introduced.

A general all-class posting can ask if anyone would like to post a devil's-advocate response advocating the other side of the question. Alternatively, the instructor can post a varied opinion. If the instructor does offer the devil's advocate position, a clear statement should be made that this is the intent of the posting. Otherwise, everyone who has been responding "I agree" may think that their position is "wrong." Let's say a yes/no type of question was asked and everyone was restating the yes position. If the instructor then posts a devil's advocate statement advocating the no position without clearly indicating that the intent is to bring out the other side of the argument, then suddenly the whole class may think they were incorrect about the yes position. It is important to remember that the instructor is a monumental authority figure to most students. This seems to be even truer in the online environment, perhaps because of the lack of voice inflection. The written word sounds like gospel where the spoken word may betray a level of uncertainty.

Down the Garden Path

Sometimes the flaw in a discussion isn't with the question itself. The discussion may just get headed down a loosely connected tangent. In that case, the instructor needs to refocus the discussion on the main topic under discussion.

Starting and Stopping the Discussion

Most courses that have facilitators also have specific start and stop dates for units. Generally these are weekly. Students should not have access to future discussions too far in advance. Opening the forum a day or two early to allow students some additional flexibility should be enough. Flexibility is a key component of online courses and one the instructor needs to keep in mind while sticking with the course deadlines.

In some programs, course assignment folders and discussions are available for the duration of the course. This always-open curriculum seems to negate the feeling of community that connects everyone. Some students have been observed rushing through everything and completing all assignments and discussions within a day or two of the course start date. Likewise, the always-open curriculum, without due dates or a late policy, allows some students to wait until the last minute to even begin working, turning in a flood of work to the instructor just before the grades are due. From the perspective of students who are following the posted course schedule, they report that they feel behind schedule when others have posted discussions and assignments before the unit was even scheduled to begin. This causes undue anxiety for those students who are on track with the course calendar.

ACCESSIBILITY

Another cause of anxiety is student inability to access parts of a course site. In chapter 3 it was stated that every tool should be evaluated to determine if it is available, operable, and accessible to the student. Once it is determined a tool will be used, the site needs to be maintained so that the tool remains available for all to use. An online student who has an assignment to post becomes very anxious when the course login page is unavailable.

In one case, the author, while teaching a beginning digital photography course, was requiring the use of an online photo album site for the posting and viewing of digital photos. The site worked for the first two to three weeks of the class. Then it became increasingly unreliable. Eventually, another site had to be found because the site closed for maintenance and was not available for several days. This period of unreliability and the need to move photos to another online site caused a great deal of stress among the students. The author had no way of knowing that the site would crash during the course. Students understood that fact. However, another solution had to be found midcourse. It took several days to realize a permanent switch to another site was needed and then it took a few more days to implement it. Even one day is a lifetime to an anxious online student!

Another side to the accessibility discussion is making sure that all parts of the course are accessible to users with disabilities. This topic is much too large for this book, but be aware that many people with disabilities take online classes to avoid some of the difficulties associated with attending a face-to-face class. It is imperative that all course materials be available in more than one format to accommodate individual needs. The online classroom should not offer as many stumbling blocks to participation as the physical classroom does for many people. The online instructor needs to know whom to call on in their institution or agency if a student reports difficulty accessing any part of the class because of a disability. A great source of information about web accessibility is WebAIM, which stands for Web Accessibility in Mind (http://www.webaim.org/).

One thing that will help people with a variety of disabilities as well as those who have expensive Internet connections is to have course materials in a format that allows easy printing. Keep in mind that many people will print course materials to be read offline. In most cases this has to do with sharing the line for the Internet connection with family members. For some people it is because reading off paper, rather than on a screen, better meets their learning style. Whatever the reason, remember that any changes to course materials need to be made before students have access to them. Otherwise they may print off the pages and be using incorrect information. If a change in materials has to be made after students have access, post announcements in several ways, including via email, to make sure students are aware of the changes.

SHARING FILES BETWEEN WINDOWS-BASED PCS AND MACINTOSH COMPUTERS

Web pages are compatible with virtually all operating systems, the two most common of which are Windows-based PCs (PCs) and Apple's Macintosh computers (Macs). This cross-platform compatibility is wonderful. The one area that can be problematic for people with different operating systems is when files are shared.

Whether students are sending assignments to the instructor or sharing them with peers, glitches can occur, especially if some people are using Macs and others are using PCs. The most common problem that occurs between the two operating systems is the way that the computer indicates the software that was used to create a document. Macs don't need to add a file extension, a punctuation mark/three letter suffix, to the file name to alert the computer about the software program used to create the file. Macintosh computers automatically encode this information into the file. When another Macintosh opens the file, it reads the code and automatically looks for the correct program with which to open the file. On the other hand, Windows-based PCs need that three-letter file extension in order to know which program to use when opening the file. Here is an example of how the same file name would appear to the computer user, depending on the type of computer on which the file was saved:

Civil War lesson plan created in MS Word on a Macintosh: CivilWarLP.

Civil War lesson plan file created in MS Word on a PC: CivilWarLP.doc.

Here are some common file extensions and the document type or program to which it refers.

.doc—Microsoft Word
.rtf—Rich Text Format
.ppt—Microsoft PowerPoint
.wpd—WordPerfect
.htm or .html—The most common webpage format
.jpg—Photograph format
.gif—Image format, usually clipart or line drawings

There are some great sources on the Internet to identify file extensions and the associated software program. Here are two good ones:

1. Almost every file format in the world (http://www.ace.net.nz/tech/TechFileFormat.html#Top)
2. WhatIs (http://whatis.techtarget.com/fileFormatA/0,289933,sid9,00.html)

If a PC user shares a file with a Mac user, there is usually no problem as long as both computers have the appropriate software program. Problems generally occur when a Mac user shares a file with a PC user. The Mac user needs to add the file extension to the file name so the PC user can open it. One way to avoid this incompatibility is to use file formats that are cross-platform such as saving files as HTML/webpages or saving them in the Rich Text Format.

Once in a while, files to be opened on a Windows-based PC from Macintosh users open as gibberish. Even when the Macintosh user carefully adds the file extension, the file can still be garbled. One tip that was a great discovery was to use the Netscape Internet browser when downloading email attachments. It turns out that Macintosh computers automatically encode files before sending them as attachments. PC computers don't always have the software to decode these files. The Netscape browser contains the software to decode the files. Therefore, a PC user accessing a web-based email account through the Netscape browser can download the email attachment and solve this encryption problem.

File-sharing problems can also occur even when all students are using the same computer platform. It is important to remember that all parties who want to view a file need to have the same software program, and sometimes the same version of the software program, to be able to open the file. It is helpful to set some software requirements, just like setting hardware requirements, before the course begins. The alternative is to make sure that all files are saved in a cross-platform, cross-program format such as HTML/web page format.

ASSISTING STUDENTS WITH NAVIGATION

Many students who are first-time online learners have a hard time figuring out the navigation of course sites. For the first few units of a course it is helpful to offer explicit directions to the materials or give students the URL for the appropriate pages via email. It is better to offer too much direction and instruction rather than not enough until students get comfortable with the course.

Some students also don't understand that links to readings or resources may take them outside the course site and into the vast beyond of the Internet. One way to help students avoid that confusion is to set up all links so that they open in a new browser window. Students will at least still have the course page open behind the current window. For some tech novices, even that may be confusing because the back button on the browser won't take them back to the course site. They don't realize it is still open behind the window they are viewing. A little instructor help here and there with technical problems led to this resulting message:

"Your support and understanding of my technologically challenged self really exhibited itself through your encouraging and honest commentaries of the work I presented. My colleagues and administrators have even noticed the difference in me as a result of taking your class. . . . I thank you for not giving up on me and for extending your knowledge to me" (A. Gallegos, personal communication, 2003).

11

Looking toward the Future

CLIMATIC CHANGES

Online instructors need to be aware of climatic changes in the online community. A sudden chill may mean that a message has been misread and the student has hurt feelings. Warming trends can bode well for the classroom environment unless things become too hot. Heated reactions can result from misunderstood messages.

Suggestions for appropriate ways to respond to these situations have already been shared. The message here is that a developing communication problem may not be obvious at first but the astute instructor can often "feel" the climate shift. That feeling should cause the teacher to be more alert when reading postings and emails, looking for possible signs of trouble.

The truth is that whenever a group of people works together, some personality and communication problems will inevitably occur. No instructor is perfect. In fact, showing that imperfection can be very healthy is evidenced in this comment made at the end of a course.

"I just want to thank you for teaching this course. I especially appreciate your willingness to improve, your teachability, your approachability, your flexibility, and your humility. It was refreshing to be taught by someone who realizes they don't know everything there is to know and who appreciates that someone else has good ideas too (especially people as ignorant about computers as us). I'm amazed that you are flexible to change and you are not only open to new ideas presented by the classmates, but you encourage it" (H. Haddox, personal communication, 2003).

INSTRUCTOR IMPROVEMENT

End-of-Course Survey

It is healthy to accept the fact that none of us is perfect. That said, it doesn't excuse the need to improve with each course. A good instructor, face-to-face or online, will seek out ways to improve both the course and the instruction. Chapter 8 discussed assessment, but one side of the assessment picture was left out. Every institution or agency should be assessing both the course and the instructor every time a class is taught. Good teachers want this feedback so that changes can be made before the course is taught the next time. If the institution/agency does an assessment, but the assessment data is so slow in arriving that it does not allow for timely changes, the instructor may need to formulate some type of feedback device. A simple end-of-course survey that asks students to provide anonymous input is very worthwhile. Many of the things noted in this book began or developed because of a comment made on an end-of-course survey. Here is a list of questions frequently used by the author to gather input after a course:

1. What did you like best about this online course?
2. What did you like least about your online learning experience? What course activity was the least helpful to you? Why?
3. What was your greatest frustration in taking this distance education course? What could be done to eliminate this frustration?
4. What was the most relevant or useful information/skill that you acquired during this course? What course activity was the most helpful to you? Why?
5. What content should be added or deleted from the course outline?
6. What improvements should be made in the instruction of the course? In what ways could the instructor have improved the course for you?
7. Briefly describe your experiences with cooperative learning during the course. How can the peer interaction/feedback process be improved?

8. What technical assistance or background would have been helpful as you were taking this workshop? How did you solve technical problems? What technical problems did you encounter?
9. Would you recommend this course to others? Why or why not?

Taking Courses

Many instructors feel that it is worthwhile to take courses to improve their teaching whether or not a survey has shown a need. Many on-ground courses that discuss teaching in general can be helpful to the online instructor. Institutions and agencies for whom the instructor teaches often have a training course for new instructors. Current instructors can ask to be included in those trainings as a review. Many institutions/agencies are also developing refresher courses for their veteran online teaching staff. In addition to in-house trainings, other opportunities exist. Some universities now offer advanced degrees in distance or online learning. An excellent program to consider is the master's in education in online teaching and learning at California State University at Hayward. More information on that program is available at http://www.online.csuhayward.edu/.

In addition to formal courses, there are opportunities at conferences for informal seminars. Most national teaching conferences have begun including sessions about online and distance education. A conference devoted specifically to distance learning topics is sponsored by the University of Wisconsin at Madison: The Annual Conference on Distance Teaching and Learning (http://www.uwex.edu/disted/conference/).

Contact with Other Instructors

An excellent informal way to improve instruction is through discussions with other online educators. Ask if the sponsoring agency or institution has a listserv or discussion forum where facilitators can discuss problems, ideas, and suggestions. If in-house discussions aren't possible, look at an online forum such as The Wellspring (http://wellspring.isinj.com/), a community devoted to distance education. Also, check out the University of Wisconsin's Distance Education Clearinghouse (http://www.uwex.edu/disted/). This web page has links to journals, forums, newsgroups, and other resources that may connect the instructor with other online teachers.

Mentors

Linking up with instructors through newsgroups and forums is helpful but sometimes a more hands-on approach is needed when working toward improvement. Some agencies offer mentor teachers to new instructors. This arrangement allows an experienced online instructor to sit in on the class being taught by a new online facilitator without actually taking part in discussions. The mentor lurks in on conversations and emails and offers ideas to the new teacher behind the scenes. Not only does the new teacher benefit, but mentors benefit through their observation of and conversations with the person they are mentoring.

TAs

All of the methods mentioned earlier are dependent on already having a job in online education. Getting some experience in distance education to be able to get an online teaching job is a new variation on an age-old problem. One method is to work as an unpaid teacher's assistant (TA) to an online educator. This offers the opportunity to participate in the online environment with a seasoned instructor. The instructor acts as a mentor while the TA gains valuable experience working in the online environment. After the course ends, the instructor can serve as a reference when the TA is applying for online positions. This is exactly how the author first got her foot in the virtual online teaching door! Thanks, Dennis!

SEE YOU ONLINE

The world of distance education is growing rapidly. Every instructor needs to give every online student the best experience possible. No book can discuss all the possible scenarios, eventualities, and duties of a profession. That is especially true when the profession is both new and evolving, as this profession is. I hope this book has offered some insights and ideas of value as you work to be the best online teacher you can be. Your online students deserve no less!

References

American Council on Education. (2000, September 11). *Fact sheet on higher education: Frequently asked questions about distance education.* Retrieved September 14, 2003, from ACE: http://www.acenet.edu/resources/fact-sheets/distance-education.pdf.

Batista, E. (2000, June 12). *Online learning's long curve.* Retrieved September 17, 2003, from Wired News: http://www.wired.com/news/business/0%2C1367%2C36847%2C00.html.

Chambers, John. (1999). Keynote speech. Las Vegas, NV.

Hall, B. (2000). *eLearning: Building competitive advantage through people and technology.* Retrieved September 14, 2003, from Forbes eLearning: http://www.forbes.com/specialsections/elearning/e-01.htm.

OnlineLearning.net. (2003). *Is online teaching for me: Self-evaluation quiz.* Retrieved August 13, 2003, from OnlineLearning.net: http://www.online-learning.net/InstructorCommunity/selfevaluation.html.

Valentine, D. (2002). Distance learning: Promises, problems, and possibilities [Electronic version]. *Online Journal of Distance Learning Administration, (V)3.* Retrieved September 14, 2003, from http://www.westga.edu/~distance/ojdla/fall53/valentine53.html.

About the Author

Kay Johnson Lehmann won the Milken National Educator Award and the Washington Award for Excellence in Education for her abilities to reach every student in the classroom. Her innovative methods use hands-on constructivist teaching with technology integration to bring social studies, reading, and other subjects alive for her middle school students. Garrison Middle School, Walla Walla, Washington, with a free-reduced lunch rate of 50 percent and a large second-language learner population, provided plenty of opportunity to use the methods shared in this book.

Summers spent working with teachers in the Bill and Melinda Gates Foundation's Teacher Leadership Project, along with a master's degree in education with a specialty in online teaching and learning, led to working full time in teacher professional development. Her online courses and face-to-face workshops feature the same constructivist, technology-enhanced methods that were so successful in the classroom.

Lehmann is the author of *Surviving Inclusion* (ScarecrowEducation, 2003). In addition, she has authored two articles as a contributor to the Microsoft Virtual Classroom Teacher Network.